The O t

Is In

By Debby Davis

The Only Way Out Is In by:
Deborah Lee Davis
Published by Davis Mission
PO Box 215
Olean, New York 14760 U.S.A.
E-mail Address: debby@davismission.com

Printed in the United States of America
ISBN: 978-0-9842416-0-6

Cover Design By:
Cathy Hoffman
Emporium, Pennsylvania

Dedication

This book is dedicated to The Lord Jesus Christ and His glorious body, my brothers and sisters in the faith. May we all learn to live in the blessings of Covenant and remain in the safety of His peace.

Table of Contents

Special Thanks

This book would not have been possible without the great help of many people. My husband Fred has labored with me as I have worked and reworked pages, making the book photo ready and helping me get it to print. My son Chris Davis spent many hours proofing some of the first pages. Bill Hoffman has listened to and read this book over and over; he has been invaluable in the formation of my thoughts and ideas. My sister Cheri has given me ideas and listened as I brainstormed. Our whole team in Africa, Spring 2009, who listened and proofed my pages as I wrote. Hannah Davis and Ruth Creveling spent hours going over the first draft. Gloria Smith labored for days on the final copy and Elaine Davis proofed the very last draft. Thank you all.

Thanks to Cathy Hoffman I have this beautiful cover which is a photo she took on one of our many mission trips together. Thank you Cathy.

Finally I want to thank everyone who encouraged me to write this book especially Lin Warner who believed in this project from the very beginning.

PREFACE

In **Luke 22:20**, Jesus offered the cup of wine to his disciples saying, "This cup is the New Covenant in my blood." Jesus didn't call it the cup of forgiveness. He called it the "New Covenant". We think of Jesus' blood as the means of forgiveness, but it is so much more than merely forgiveness. It is the *New* Covenant, which is a Covenant of Grace. The Old Covenant, under the Law of Moses, provided forgiveness. The New Covenant grants grace. Interestingly, the only way out of the old Covenant is into the new.[1]

Once you enter into the New Covenant with Jesus, you have entered into God's house. If you have not entered into God's house, if you have not become His child, then you have never entered into the New Covenant and sin and death control you. **Romans 2:4** shows, that it is God's kindness **(Ephesians 2:7)**, goodness, and grace, that led us to repentance. It is this kind of grace that comforts us at the cross of Christ and where we discover that we have nothing of value to offer Jesus in return for his precious blood sacrifice. Yet it is His grace that speaks louder than our sin and says, "Come let us make a Covenant together. I'll willingly trade my life for yours."

This, my friend, is the New Covenant. It is a life exchange with Almighty God. May we ever be attentive to this Covenant. May we guard, cherish, and protect it at any cost, for it is wonderful and amazing! Let us walk into God's house. If you have never made this step, the only way out of fear, depression, feelings of worthlessness, loneliness, or anxiety, is in! If you have broken your covenants and need to return to God's house, the only way out is in. Everything within you may say run the other way, don't even try to enter the house. However, God, our loving Heavenly Father, is standing just inside the door beckoning, "Come in. Let us make a Covenant together."

> **Jeremiah 31:31-34** "Behold, the days are coming, says the LORD, when I will make a **new Covenant** with the house of Israel and the house of Judah, not like the Covenant which I made with their fathers when I took them by the hand to bring them out of the land of Egypt, my Covenant which they broke, though I was their husband, says the LORD. But this is the Covenant which I will make with the house of Israel after those days, says the LORD: I will put my law within them, and I will write it upon their hearts; and I will be their God, and they shall be my people." RSV

Blessings In The House

"And if you obey the voice of the LORD your God, being careful to do all his commandments which I command you this day, the LORD your God will set you high above all the nations of the earth.

And all these blessings shall come upon you and overtake you, if you obey the voice of the LORD your God.

Blessed shall you be in the city, and blessed shall you be in the field.

Blessed shall be the fruit of your body, and the fruit of your ground, and the fruit of your beasts, the increase of your cattle, and the young of your flock.

Blessed shall be your basket and your kneading-trough.

Blessed shall you be when you come in, and blessed shall you be when you go out.

"The LORD will cause your enemies who rise against you to be defeated before you; they shall come out against you one way, and flee before you seven ways.

The LORD will command the blessing upon you in your barns, and in all that you undertake; and he will bless you

in the land which the LORD your God gives you.

The LORD will establish you as a people holy to himself, as he has sworn to you, if you keep the commandments of the LORD your God, and walk in his ways.

And all the peoples of the earth shall see that you are called by the name of the LORD; and they shall be afraid of you.

And the LORD will make you abound in prosperity, in the fruit of your body, and in the fruit of your cattle, and in the fruit of your ground, within the land which the LORD swore to your fathers to give you.

The LORD will open to you his good treasury the heavens, to give the rain of your land in its season and to bless all the work of your hands; and you shall lend to many nations, but you shall not borrow.

And the LORD will make you the head, and not the tail; and you shall tend upward only, and not downward; if you obey the commandments of the LORD your God, which I command you this day, being careful to do them,

And if you do not turn aside from any of the words which I command you this day, to the right hand or to the left, to go after other gods to serve them.

Deuteronomy 28:1-14 RSV

Chapter 1
The Gift

Yesterday had been such a difficult day. Walking for hours upon hours in the hot sun, Mark wondered if the day would ever end. Last week his father died. With his last breath he told Mark to go live with Thad. Thad was his father's oldest and dearest friend. "Don't be afraid son," the dying man said. "Thad will take care of you. I have already sent word to him and he is expecting you."

Then last night, halfway into Mark's journey, Thad arrived riding on the finest horse Mark had ever seen. Now, today, Mark himself was riding that magnificent beast. What a wonderful surprise. The young man hadn't expected his father's friend to meet him on the journey but he was glad he had. Mark smiled as he remarked about the beauty of the horse. Thad declared that the horse was the finest in the land. "A purebred," he said. "There's not another horse like it. Worth a year's wages." Mark couldn't begin to comprehend what it was like to own something that costly.

They rode until they came to an oasis. Thad was a wealthy merchant who lived at the oasis and upon their arrival there was an abundance of commotion. The master had come home. Thad immediately ordered a sacrifice be made in honor of the young man. While Mark and Thad stood outside of the camp, servants quickly led the great horse to the doorway of Thad's tent. There they laid the beast down and slit his throat. "No!" cried Mark. "Not the beautiful horse!"

Thad, ignoring Mark's obvious discomfort, took him by the hand and asked him to step over the bloody threshold into Thad's tent. Mark obeyed, his eyes wide as he entered the tent. He understood, as did everyone else, the significance of this sacrifice. Thad had offered the best he had for the young man.

He who enters a Covenant door, is considered to be the best of friends, welcomed into the house and given all of the blessings of Covenant.

Mark didn't feel worthy. After all, he was only a young man. Why such a great sacrifice? As Mark entered the tent he understood that, because of the sacrifice, Thad was offering Mark all the blessings of sonship. Thad had sacrificed the best he had for the sake of the son of his old friend. Now, through the mystery of Covenant, Mark was Thad's son and Thad would protect the lad with everything the old man owned. Everything Thad had was at Mark's disposal. The orphaned son was no longer alone. He had a new father and a new home. [1]

Have you ever heard the old proverb, "back door guests are always the best?" We understand this to mean that only one's closest friends come in the back door, while all other visitors must be formally received at the front. However, in many cultures, both ancient and contemporary, that proverb just isn't true. In some parts of the world there isn't even a back door to enter. This is because the front door threshold represents a special Covenant offered to anyone entering through it. He who enters a Covenant door, is considered to be the best of friends, welcomed into the house and given all of the blessings of Covenant.

According to H. Clay Trumble, in his book *The Threshold Covenant,* people from before the days of Abraham made Covenants by offering a sacrifice at the front door of their dwelling whether it was a tent, cave, or stone structure. This sacrifice, usually a valued animal, was placed upon the threshold and killed allowing the blood to flow across the entrance. It was the symbol of undying love, loyalty and friendship. Anyone offering such a Covenant did so knowing that this act was a promise to give the ultimate sacrifice of his life for his guest, if necessary.

Once a guest stepped over the blood-covered threshold, the Covenant bound the guest and the head of the house by the strictest laws of hospitality. Only by stepping over the blood was the Covenant sealed. Anyone coming into the house by another way was considered a threat or danger to the household.[2] We see this principle illustrated by Jesus in **John 10:1** where He said, "Verily, verily, I say unto you, He that *enters* not by the door into the sheepfold, but *climbs* up some other way, the same is a thief and a robber". (Emphasis added) There was only one right way to enter the house, and that was through the front door stepping over the bloody threshold.

In ancient Middle Eastern cultures, it was rare for a homeowner to place a guard at the front of their house. A guard was necessary only if the home had a back door or window. The reason? Everyone, even a thief, understood that coming through the front door meant a Covenant was made. Even if a sacrifice had not just been offered, many had been in the past, and therefore the front door-threshold was sacred, and demanded respect for the Covenant. In every Covenant, there are both benefits and curses. Thieves feared the curse. They would not enter through the door and then violate the home. Anyone who entered the house was offered an amazing gift, i.e. the exchange of his life for the one offering the sacrifice. With no guard at the front door, technically anyone wishing to come under the terms of this Covenant, could enter. As soon as they did they were committed to this exchange.

> **Psalms 84:10** For a day in Your courts *is* better than a thousand. I would rather be a doorkeeper in the house of my God than dwell in the tents of wickedness. NKJV

The Psalmist David longed to live in the Covenant place of God. In **Psalms 84:10** he said that the highest calling, the most desired place, the one thing that would make his life complete, would be a doorkeeper in the house of God. Throughout the Bible we see many references to doors, entryways, and thresholds. The threshold was the first thing you stepped over as you passed through the doorway and was often called the corner stone or foundation stone. Since doors are so common, most people never realize the significance of these Biblical passages. Nevertheless, they are very significant. They are the very entrance to Covenant. Jesus said in **John 14:6** that He is the

Anyone who entered the house was offered an amazing gift, i.e. the exchange of his life for the one offering the sacrifice..

only way to see God, and in **John 10:7-9,** Jesus also refers to Himself as "The Door."[3] Jesus is the entrance to eternal life, victory, and peace. He says that He is the door because we have to enter *through* Him much like we enter through a doorway. In this, Jesus is the threshold, or the cornerstone. We have to go "through" Jesus to enter into salvation.

Jesus is the entrance to eternal life, victory, and peace.

Once we enter into covenant by believing in Jesus, we pass over the threshold and into the household of God. In this house, we have direct access to God Almighty. He provides for us and protects us, never turning us away but giving us a future and a hope.

Ephesians 2:19-20 So then you are no longer strangers and sojourners, but you are fellow citizens with the saints and members of the **household of God**, built upon the foundation of the apostles and prophets, Christ Jesus himself being the **cornerstone**, RSV

Without passing through Jesus, The Door, The Cornerstone, Our Foundation, we cannot see God.[4] This is where we begin. However, before we can begin this journey with God, the sacrifice must be found and killed on the threshold. The blood must run from side to side, leaving no way to enter except over the flow. We are obligated to step over the blood of the sacrifice to enter into the household of God. Jesus was that perfect sacrifice and before we could enter into the house of God, His blood had to flow. As we step over the life-blood of Christ and cross the threshold into the house of God, we Covenant with God and we enter into a life for life relationship.

Isaiah 54:8 ...with everlasting love I will have compassion on you, says the LORD, your Redeemer. RSV

Isaiah 54:10 For the mountains may depart and the

> hills be removed, but my steadfast love shall not depart from you, and my Covenant of peace shall not be removed, says the LORD, who has compassion on you. RSV

Our daughter Marie-Louise was an orphan from the West African country of Côte d'Ivoire. Her mother died and six-year-old Marie was left in the care of a poor relative. The little girl missed her mom and often felt very alone. I first heard about her from our friend, Pastor Paul, and his wife. God spoke to me that Marie-Louise was to be my daughter, so my husband Fred and I began to consider adoption. I have often wondered what it must have been like for Marie-Louise when we, complete strangers, came into her life. We took her to our home, and as soon as she entered, we knew she was staying. We filled out all of the necessary papers for legal adoption. She stepped over our threshold and into our hearts. She has all of the blessings and obligations of Covenant. We provide love, food, and housing and she has to clean her room. She is our daughter and because we are American citizens, she is now also an American citizen. Her American passport proves that a Covenant was made. She has all of the benefits, rights, and responsibilities as a United States citizen. And she is protected by the best America has to offer.

As we step over the life-blood of Christ and cross the threshold into the house of God, we Covenant with God and we enter into a life for life relationship.

When we first became missionaries in Abidjan, Côte d'Ivoire, our friend Marie, who worked for the American Embassy, asked us for our passports. She informed us that we needed to register our names and addresses with the American Consulate. We did this and a few years later when a coup d'état war broke out, the Embassy staff immediately contacted us. Because we were

Once a guest stepped over the blood-covered threshold, the Covenant bound the guest and the head of the house by the strictest laws of hospitality. Only by stepping over the blood was the Covenant sealed.

United States citizens, the Embassy would send us food and water if the city were shut down in the event of war or civil unrest. They would even bring armored cars to our home and pick us up if we needed to be evacuated. All of this was because we held American passports. Now our adopted daughter, Marie-Louise had the same privileges. American servicemen, stationed in Côte d'Ivoire, would gladly lay down their lives for her because of the paper she had declaring that a Covenant had been made between the United States of America and our daughter.

Just like Marie-Louise and Mark, from the story at the beginning of this chapter, we too were all orphaned. Lost in sin, we wandered alone until one day Jesus came and found us. He took us to his home and there He offered the greatest of all gifts, His own life as a sacrifice for us. He asks us to step over the blood and receive His sacrifice. In doing so, we accept this wonderful Covenant, exchanging our life of suffering and sin for His life full of hope and peace. We have a new father and a new home. Everything He has is now ours as well. We have become citizens of Heaven. The only way out of our loneliness and sin is by coming into the House of God. We guard in our hearts the passport of grace, purchased by the blood of Jesus Christ. Everything we need He will supply.

> **1 John 3:1a, 2b** "Behold what manner of love the Father has bestowed on us, that we should be called children of God! "Beloved, now we are children of God; NKJV

Romans 8:16-17a "The Spirit Himself bears witness with our spirit that we are children of God, and if children, then heirs - heirs of God and joint heirs with Christ, NKJV

Once we enter into covenant by believing in Jesus, we pass over the threshold and into the household of God. In this house we have direct access to God Almighty. He provides for us and protects us, never turning us away but giving us a future and a hope.

Chapter 2
In The House

Psalms 5:7 But as for me, I will come into Your house in the multitude of Your mercy; In fear of You I will worship toward Your holy temple. NKJV

A young shepherd was taking care of sheep when his father told him to go to the military camp where his brothers were preparing to fight against their enemies. “Take some food to your brothers,” his father said. “While you are there, find out how the battle is going and bring me news.”

Gathering provisions he quickly obeyed his father. Just as he arrived at the camp, the biggest man he had ever seen stood across the valley and began to curse the Israelites. “Give me a man to fight,” the giant repeated over and over. Not believing his own ears, David began to ask everyone who was this blasphemer, and how did he dare insult the army of the living God in this way? The giant, whose name was Goliath, had been coming like this for the last forty days and everyone in the camp was scared, nervous, and afraid.

Feeling shame for his country, because Goliath had insulted the Living God, and because no one seemed to be willing to fight the accuser, David became outraged. He said that something needed to be done to take away this humiliation. Who did this uncircumcised Philistine think he was, insulting the people of Israel? How could everyone just stand there while he insulted the army of the Living God? David was indignant, and he asked those standing around, "What does King Saul have to say about this?" They all gave David the same answer. "To the man who kills the giant, the king will give great riches. He will also be given the king's daughter in marriage and be free from taxes."

David found it hard to believe that anyone would allow this giant to go on taunting like this day after day. He spoke to so many people about the situation, that the king heard about the young man and called for him to come into his presence. David said to the king, "Don't let anyone be afraid any longer. I will go and fight this uncircumcised giant."

"You?" the king asked. "You are just a boy. The men here are all seasoned warriors and have been fighting since they were young. What makes you think you can go fight this giant when even my best soldiers are afraid?"

With a look of determination, David began to tell of the times he had rescued his father's sheep. He had fought and killed both a lion and a bear. He finished by saying, "This uncircumcised Philistine shall be like them."

Often people ask me why David continued to refer to Goliath as uncircumcised? David was referring to the Blood Covenant that the people of Israel had with God, through their father Abraham. For the Hebrews, circumcision was the sign of that Covenant. Unlike the children of Abraham, Goliath had never been circumcised and hence he was not in this Covenant. The Covenant of Abraham was the doorway into God's household. It offered many blessings, which included protection, prosperity, and friendship, with the Lord God Almighty (Genesis 17).

David, in **Psalms 91,** called this Covenant, "Abiding under the shadow of the Almighty" or "living under the protection of God's roof". Those who come under God's roof, entering through the Covenant, become God's children, therefore receiving all of the benefits of family. Goliath had never entered into this Covenant. He was not a child of promise and was defiantly not dwelling under the "Shadow of the Almighty". As such, he had no power over the children of Abraham. It seemed that everyone had forgotten the Covenant except for David. They had forgotten the fact that Goliath had no right or authority to hurl insults at them. They allowed the giant's enormous size and menacing words to put fear into their hearts. David, on the other hand, was not afraid, because he understood the power of Israel's Covenant with God. Israel belonged in God's family and therefore God was obligated to protect them at any cost.

The Covenant of Abraham was the doorway into God's household. It offered many blessings, which included protection, prosperity, and friendship, with the Lord God Almighty .

After King Saul gave him permission to fight, David began to prepare for the battle. Taking only his staff, slingshot, and five smooth stones, he went to face the giant. As David approached the battleground, the giant mocked, "Am I a dog, that a boy would come to fight me?" Insulted and angry, Goliath declared he would kill David and feed his flesh to the vultures.

David knew that his Covenant obligation was to love God with all of his heart, and as a result he became known as a man after God's own heart.

Looking up at Goliath, little David said, "You come against me with all your mighty weapons of war, but I come in the name of the Lord of hosts. It is this God and His army that you have insulted. Today the Lord will give you to me, and I will kill you. I will cut off your head and feed your body to the birds and wild animals. Then all the world will know that there is a God in Israel and that this battle belongs to Him!"

Running towards the giant, David slung one of his stones and struck the giant on the forehead, causing him to fall to the ground. David ran to the still living giant, and snatching his enemy's own sword, chopped off the massive head.

It wasn't only the force of the stone that brought down this giant. David acknowledged the giant's weapons of war, but David was coming with more than that, he was coming armed with the name of the Lord of hosts. Not only did the giant die that day, but encouraged by David's bravery, the entire army of Israel pursued their enemies, killing over thirty thousand of the uncircumcised Philistines. It was a miraculous day as the situation turned around giving Israel complete victory.[1] Everyone knew that there was a God in Israel and that He was the Almighty God. Not only that, but they also knew that David had a personal relationship with that God.

Throughout David's life, he made many Covenants, and was known for being a man of Covenant. As an example, he made them with God, the Prophet Samuel, King Saul, Saul's son Jonathan, Uriah, and even with some of his enemies. David understood the terms of Covenant and lived by them.

Moses, in the book of Deuteronomy explained the conditions of Covenant for the Children of Abraham.[2] Moses said that man's obligations were very easy. A man should love the Lord, walk in His ways, and keep His word. God's responsibility in this Covenant included the promise of prosperity, an increase in both their families and herds, and protection. If they were ever attacked, God would cause the enemy to flee in seven directions.[3] When he became Moses' successor, Joshua reaffirmed these promises and obligations of the Covenant.[4]

David knew that his Covenant obligation was to love God with all of his heart, and as a result, he became known as a man after God's own heart.[5] David was in a Covenant with God, and had entered into God's house, coming under the protection of God Almighty's roof. He knew that he was God's child and was not afraid of this enemy. David made a life exchange with the Almighty and was committed to the Covenant. Therefore he reaped the blessings of his Covenants. We may never be able to completely measure the depths of Covenant. We may never know how deep and how wide this wonderful and mysterious Covenant is. Yet, like David we may experience it.[6]

We may never know how deep and how wide this wonderful and mysterious Covenant is. Yet, like David we may experience it.

Jesus further explained the terms of Covenant in **Mark**

12:28-31. When asked by the Pharisees, "What is the greatest commandment?" He responded with, "Love the Lord your God with all of your heart, your mind, and your strength." He then added, "The second is like it, Love your neighbor as yourself."[7]

Jesus finished his discourse by saying, "You now have my name. Anything you ask of the Father in my name He shall give to you." Just like the disciples, when we come into a Covenant with God it changes who we are and even changes our name.

When Jesus celebrated the Blood Covenant ceremony of Holy Communion, (discussed in detail in my book *Keepers of Salt*) Jesus finished his discourse by saying, "You now have my name. Anything you ask of the Father in my name He shall give to you." Just like the disciples, when we come into a Covenant with God it changes who we are and even changes our name. I took my husband's name when I entered into the Covenant of marriage with him. Because of our Covenant with Marie-Louise, our adopted daughter, she now has our family name. David took issue with Goliath, because the Giant had called God's people "The army of Saul". David said we are not called by the name of King Saul, we are the Army of the Lord of Hosts and he knew the power of Covenant that came with that name.

Goliath taunted the Israelites every day. He intimidated them with merely his size and his words. David knew the provisions of their Covenant and the power of God's name. He knew that if he would come to the battlefield that God would be there and fight for him. When we understand the Covenant, we understand that our problems are not just our problem alone. They belong to God. You had a life exchange when you stepped over the blood and entered into

God's house. You came to live "Under the Shadow of The Almighty". The battles you face are no longer your sole responsibility. You are not alone in your troubles. You live in God's house and according to the terms of the Covenant, God is obligated to fight for you.

> **Ephesians 2:11-13** Wherefore remember, that ye being in time past Gentiles in the flesh, who are called Uncircumcision by that which is called the Circumcision in the flesh made by hands; That at that time ye were without Christ, being aliens from the commonwealth of Israel, and strangers from the covenants of promise, having no hope, and without God in the world: But now in Christ Jesus ye who sometimes were far off are made nigh by the blood of Christ. KJV

Paul, the author of **Ephesians 2:11-12,** said that we were once called uncircumcised. We were excluded from the benefits of the Covenant. We were strangers to the Covenants of promise. We were without God and without hope. However, in verse thirteen, Paul continues to say that we have been brought "nigh" or brought to the door of God's house through the sacrificial blood of Jesus.[8] We are also members of the Covenant and are of God's household. Praise the Lord! Since we have been adopted into God's house, we now have all the benefits of sonship. We walked through the door of God's house, stepped over the sacrificial blood of Jesus, and became sons and daughters of God.

The battles you face are no longer your sole responsibility. You are not alone in your troubles. You live in God's house and according to the terms of the Covenant, God is obligated to fight for you.

> **Ephesians 2:19** Now therefore ye are no more strangers and foreigners, but fellow citizens with the saints, and of the household of God. KJV

Like David, facing Goliath, situations come against us. Our accusers shout words of defeat and discouragement. Things like, "You can't make it, and your life is too hard. There is never enough money and your marriage will never survive. You will always be sick. You will never be good enough. You are a nothing, and a nobody, no one cares, wants, or even loves you."

Have faith in the Covenant. God will fight for you. He will bring solutions to your problems. He will heal your body and provide for all of your needs.

Who is your giant? Is it sickness? Have you been sick for so long you don't even remember what it was like to be well? Could it be that a dead-end job laughs at you every-day when you go to work? Is your marriage in trouble and you can't see an end to your difficulties? Are your children a constant worry? Jesus' sacrificial blood paid the price for your healing, your poverty, your marriage problems, and your heartaches. Look at each of these situations like David did Goliath. Face your problems and speak to them saying, "Problem, you are uncircumcised. I live in the house of God and my problems are not my own. You are not insulting me; you are insulting the Living God. He will fight for me." Throw these words, like stones, at your giant. Have faith in the Covenant. God will fight for you. He will bring solutions to your problems. He will heal your body and provide for all of your needs. We can have and experience the peace, joy, assurance, confidence, and power of Covenant.

Incidentally, do you want to know why David had to cut off Goliath's head? He did this to stop the giant from talking. When you allow God to fight for you, he will stop the mouth of your accusers. They no longer have anything to say. You are a child of Almighty God. Who are these who dare speak against the children of the Living God? Like David, face your enemy and tell him, "I come against you in the name of the Lord God Almighty." When you do this, your enemy has nothing more to say. Because of your faith, and the victory God brings in your life, all the earth will know that there is a God who lives in you.

I Samuel 17:46 This day the LORD will deliver you into my hand, and I will strike you down, and cut off your head; and I will give the dead bodies of the host of the Philistines this day to the birds of the air and to the wild beasts of the earth; that all the earth may know that there is a God in Israel, RSV

Like David, face your enemy and tell him, "I come against you in the name of the Lord God Almighty.

THE ONLY WAY OUT IS IN

Chapter 3

A Prisoner of Love

Philemon 1:9 Yet for love's sake I rather beseech thee, being such an one as Paul the aged, and now also a prisoner of Jesus Christ. KJV

Elizabeth looked forward to this day, ever since she could remember. When she was just a child, she and her mother had been sold into slavery to pay her father's debt. "Twenty years," her mother used to say. All they had to do was work hard for the Ben-Simon family. In twenty years they would have paid the debt. Then sickness came, and her mother needed a doctor and medicine. Elizabeth borrowed more money from master Ben-Simon. For Elizabeth, the twenty years soon became thirty and then thirty-five.

Finally today she was free.

Elizabeth was now almost forty years old. A whole lifetime had gone by, and sadly, Elizabeth's mother did not live long enough to celebrate this day with her daughter.

With all of her memories blurred together, Elizabeth tried to remember life before the Ben-Simons. Trying as hard as she could, she just couldn't remember her father. She could remember Sarah; she was the youngest child in her former master's home. Elizabeth could even remember the day she was born. What a cute baby she was. Playmates, friends, enemies, they had been all three, sometimes at the same time. Now Sarah was all grown up and had a family of her own. Elizabeth visited them just yesterday.

The Ben-Simons were good to Elizabeth. But today she was free. Free to go where? Suddenly freedom didn't seem like such a good idea after all. Where would she go? Her mother was gone and her father, well, no one had heard from him in decades. She had no other life. No place to go. She loved the Ben-Simons. They were her only "family".

"Sir," Elizabeth said as she approached her former master. "I would like to speak with you if I may." How should she say what she wanted to say? The fear of being rejected was beginning to rise up in her throat and choke her. Would she be forced to leave? she wondered. Master Ben-Simon nodded and she continued, "I don't have any place to go. You are my only family now. I don't want to leave. I will work for you, for nothing if you like, only please don't make me go."

> **Deuteronomy 15:16-17** "And if it happens that he says to you, `I will not go away from you,' because he loves you and your house, since he prospers with you, then you shall take an awl and thrust *it* through his ear

> to the door, and he shall be your servant forever. Also to your female servant you shall do likewise." KJV

With a look of love and a kind smile Master Ben-Simon replied, "Do you know what you are asking? Do you understand that if we do this, there is no going back?" He waited until she nodded and then continued. "Good, I will call everyone together and meet you at the door."

It wasn't long before there was a crowd gathered around the entrance of the Ben-Simon's grand home. There were men from town, friends, children, grandchildren, and other slaves who had come to be witnesses of this event. Everyone was there to observe the Covenant making. Master Ben-Simon declared, "Elizabeth has vowed that she desires to stay with us. She has chosen to remain a servant in our house for the rest of her life. Come close everyone, and witness her Covenant to us."

With that said, he motioned for Elizabeth to stand in the front doorway of the Ben-Simon mansion. She leaned her head against the frame of the door and closed her eyes. Would it hurt she wondered? It was over almost before she knew it. Master Ben-Simon had pierced through her ear with a sharp metal object, used to bore leather, penetrating right into the doorframe. The pain was intense, but when she saw the looks of love on everyone's face, the pain didn't seem so important. For years she felt like a slave but today she felt something different. The past was gone. The rejection she always felt in her heart from her dad's absence disappeared. She felt healed inside. No longer a slave by force; she loved and was loved in return. She was now a prisoner of hope and of love. Finally she had a future and she belonged to someone.

> **Exodus 21:5-6** And if the servant shall plainly say, I love my master, my wife, and my children; I will not go out free: Then his master shall bring him unto the judges; he shall also bring him to the door, or unto the door post; and his master shall bore his ear through with an awl; and he shall serve him for ever. KJV

This story seems extraordinary to those of us who live in Western cultures, but it was common for those in the Mediterranean world who lived during and after the days of Moses. The Law of Moses provided for a slave who wished to remain with his master. Two things were important for a person to become a voluntary life-slave. First, he or she had to come to the front door of the master's home, for it was the place where Covenants were made.[1] Second, the ear of the former slave had to be pierced allowing blood from the pierced ear to flow. Both the door and the ear were constant reminders of the Covenant, the door with a mark from the awl and possibly blood and pieces of flesh, and also the ear with its hole, large enough to leave a lasting scar on the slave.

We have now made a life exchange, our life for His. This exchange is the result of a circumcised heart.

Compare the symbolism of Elizabeth having her ear pierced, signifying her Covenant of life service, and our heart being circumcised, signifying our Covenant with God. The Apostle Paul understood circumcision. He explained that our heart is circumcised when it is pierced, or when it is convinced of sin.[2] He also said, that the real power of the Covenant, is that the love of God is divinely poured into the hearts of His people.[3] Love being the motivating factor in the Covenant.

The psalmist David described this special relationship in

Psalms 34:18 and Psalms 51:17, as having a broken and contrite spirit.[4] David makes it clear that the heart and spirit are one. The Bible says that Jesus is knocking at the door of your heart, your place of Covenant.[5] He longs for you to let Him step over your threshold and into your heart. A circumcised heart acknowledges the need for a redeemer. We then enter into a Covenant relationship, by accepting the sacrificial blood of Jesus, making Him our Covenant Redeemer. We have now made a life exchange, our life for His. This exchange is the result of a circumcised heart.

My father has always been a dog lover. Since he loves dogs, it was not a surprise when a neighbor called and asked him to take an unwanted dog. The man was going on a trip and left the unwanted dog tied up behind his barn. My father went that afternoon to get the dog. Walking behind the man's barn, my dad heard a noise that made his hair stand on end. The poor animal didn't bark, but growled and snarled as my father approached. On close inspection, he could see that the dog had been tied by a chain attached to a pole on a slab of concrete. Since his food dish was chewed beyond recognition, there was no water in sight and the whole area smelled badly, it was obvious that the poor thing had been this way for many days.

Not knowing how best to approach the snarling dog, Dad threw his coat over its head so that he could unhook the chain from the pole without getting bit. Grabbing the now released chain, he tried to pull the dog after him, but the snarling beast resisted going beyond the boundaries of his concrete prison. The dog pulled on that chain unsuccessfully for so long, he now believed he couldn't go past the concrete. Finally, after a good tug, Dad won and dragged the dog to his truck. After arriving at our farm, my father tried to take the chain off. Great was his surprise when the chain wouldn't budge. There was no leather collar only chain, and links from that chain were firmly embedded into the neck of the dog. It was no wonder that the dog didn't think he could leave the concrete slab. He pulled on that chain for so long that it was now a part of him.

My dad soon realized that the dog's neck with the embedded chain was painful and full of infection. If he didn't get it out, it would eventually kill the dog. Link by link Father worked at the chain. Gently he would wiggle and tug at the imbedded metal, careful so as not to cause the dog unnecessary pain. Whimpering now and then, the dog seemed to know that Dad was trying to help him. Soon my father was done. After pouring some ointment into the wounds, he let the dog lie and rest unchained on the barn floor. The next morning the dog was gone.

The real power of the covenant, is that the love of God is divinely poured into the hearts of His people.

My whole family began searching for the dog. We found him out in the cow pasture looking towards the farmhouse. For days the dog stayed out in the pasture longing for food yet fearful to come too close. My father could not catch him or coax him to come to the house. Every day Dad would feed his other dogs and leave extra food for him, but the dog would never come and eat until after my dad left. Day after day, my dad would call him to come but the dog was still afraid. Then one day the poor creature gathered enough courage to come into the yard as the others were being fed. After many days, Dad actually touched the dog, reaching out his hand and patting his head.

It wasn't long before the dog would come running whenever he saw my dad. He played with the dog every day, and he noticed that the dog's neck had finally begun to heal. "Someday soon I'll have to get you a real collar," he told the dog. The next time he went to town he did just that. Gathering the dog to him, Dad put a beautiful leather collar around the dog's neck. The collar was complete with a shiny new tag engraved with a note that declared that the dog belonged to my dad.

Oftentimes when God begins to work on our lives, we think He is against us, even trying to kill us... While it may seem as if God is trying to destroy us, in truth, He is giving us new life.

Dad began to train the dog to hunt and soon he was the best in the pack. Whenever he would go to town the dog would jump into the truck, sitting right next to him. If he took the car and other passengers, the dog would reluctantly sit in the back seat, but stretch his neck to rest his head upon Dad's shoulder.

Where before the dog had resisted and strained to get away from a cruel master, to the point of making the torturous chains a part of him, now he was straining to get closer to a master whom he loved. Now fastened by love, the most powerful attachment of all, nothing could entice the dog to leave. He had grown to love my dad. He was a prisoner of love.

I have often wondered about that old dog. He must have thought that my dad was trying to kill him, and in sheer terror, he ran away. However the opposite was true, rather than killing the dog, my father was giving the dog back his life. With each link of chain that was taken out, the dog was brought closer to health.

This principle is also true for you and me. Oftentimes when God begins to work on our lives, we think He is against us,

Nevertheless, the day comes when we realize that we want to be close to Him because He alone is our future and our life, making us prisoners of hope and of love.

even trying to kill us. Link by link He takes bad things out. He knows that we need to be set free from anger, selfishness, pride, and the like. While it may seem as if God is trying to destroy us, in truth, He is giving us new life. Resisting God because of the pain, we run, hoping that we can "eat of the gospel" but without getting too close to God. Nevertheless, the day comes when we realize that we want to be close to Him because He alone is our future and our life, making us prisoners of hope and of love.

Many times the apostle Paul declared that he was a prisoner of the Lord Jesus Christ.[6] Paul's slavery was not that of a cruel master, but like Elizabeth, was voluntarily brought about by love and affection. Because Paul's heart had been convicted of his need for the sacrificial blood of Jesus, he made a Covenant with God, forever binding him by the strongest of chains, love.

Satan, the enemy of our souls is a wicked and cruel master. He has chained many to despair and depression. Do you struggle day after day wondering if you will ever be set free? Have you given up trying to escape and have you come to the conclusion that you will be bound forever? Do your past experiences make you even question the reality of a good and loving God? Perhaps you have been set free like my dad's dog, but you are afraid to be separated from your former more familiar life, and you fear new relationships. Or even more, perhaps there are links from your past so deeply embedded in your life, that you think they will be a part of you forever. Standing off to the side you yearn for love and acceptance, but fear keeps you away.

Zechariah 9:11-12 "As for you also, Because of the blood of your Covenant, I will set your prisoners free from the waterless pit. Return to the stronghold, You prisoners of hope. Even today I declare That I will restore double to you. NKJV

The prophet Zechariah foretold, in chapter nine, the coming of the New Covenant. Calling those who come to God prisoners of hope, he paints for us a picture. Using the word "hope" he illustrates a different kind of bondage. No longer drowning in a pit or sea of despair, this prisoner has hope. He now has a future brought about because of the blood of the Covenant. Not satisfied with only the promise of freedom, the prophet goes on to say that restoration comes to those who return to God. Coming back into right Covenant relationship with God restores double what has been lost. Stand aside no longer, come back to the Loving Master, The Lord God Almighty. He desires to restore you, giving to you double grace, double hope, and double love.

Psalms 68:6 God sets the solitary in families; He brings out those who are bound into prosperity; But the rebellious dwell in a dry *land.* NKJV

Coming back into right Covenant relationship with God restores double what has been lost. Stand aside no longer, come back to the Loving Master.

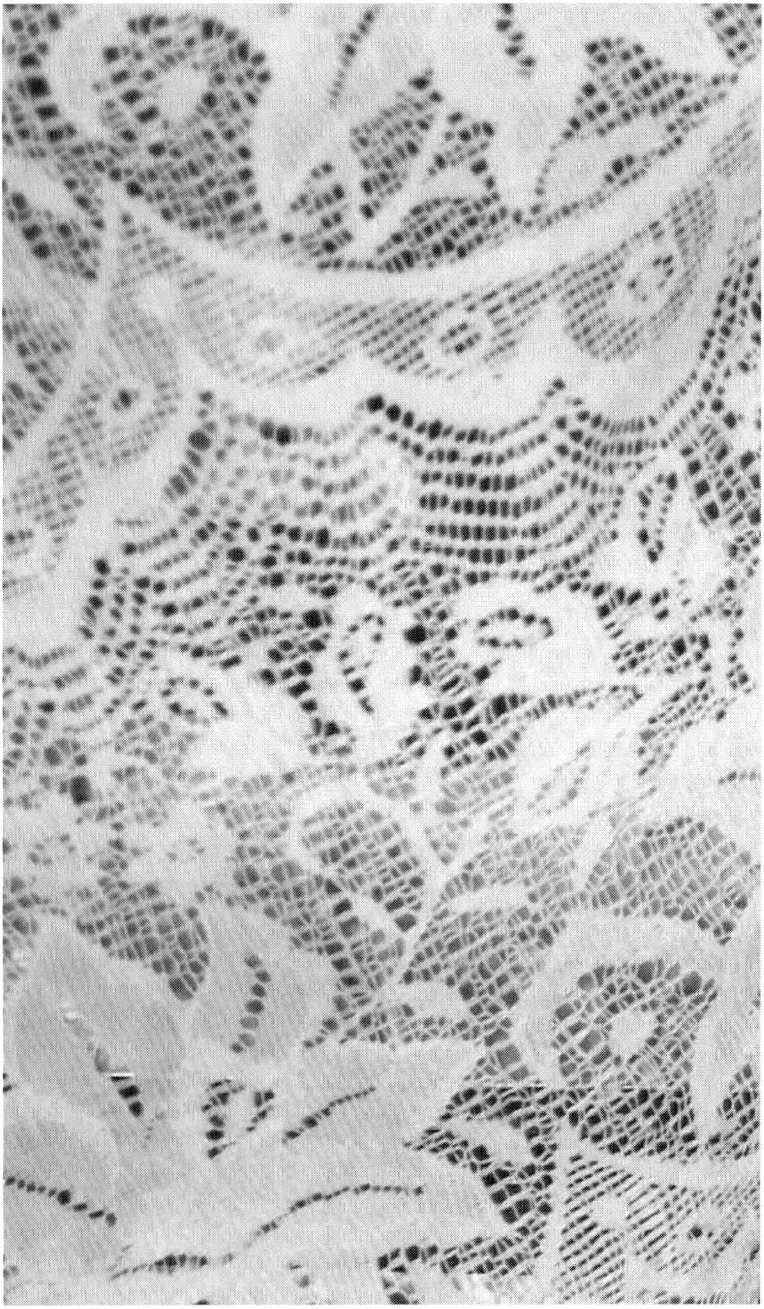

Chapter 4
And The Blood Flows

John 7:38 He that believeth on me, as the scripture hath said, out of his belly shall flow rivers of living water. KJV

Dreams can be very real and this one was no different. The house was strangely quiet. No one seemed to be there except my mom and dad, my husband Fred, and me. We were all upstairs in my grandparent's bedroom, when suddenly a banging came from the front door. The house was large, with a wide staircase stopping before the front door. My dad and Fred went down the stairs to see who or what was making all the noise. As they proceeded to open the door, a powerful presence tried to enter. Because this was a dream,

I knew that this was the devil himself. Fred and my dad alone could not push him back outside. So in answer to their cries for help, my mom and I knelt at my grandmother's bed and began to pray. As we prayed, blood began to flow. It started slowly, but soon it was a mighty river that rushed out from under the bed, across the room, and down the staircase. At the moment we started to pray, the devil had entered the house and was trying to climb the stairs, even though Fred and my dad were fighting him. I noticed that my dad and Fred could stand in the river of blood as it flowed. In and out, around their legs it swirled. However the devil could not stand in the now raging river and it carried him out of the house.

An old hymn, written by *William Cowper* in the late 1700's, says, "There is a fountain filled with blood. Flowing from Emanuel's veins. And sinners plunge beneath that flood. Lose all their guilty stains." Jesus is our threshold and from Him the River of Life originates. Earliest men, when building their homes, would first erect an altar. On this altar they would offer a sacrifice, invoking their god to live with them and protect them. This place was commonly known as the cornerstone or threshold.[1] It is through Jesus our threshold, that we enter into the house of God and come under the protection of God's roof. It is also through Jesus, the source of the River of Life, that deliverance and healing flow. The idea, of blood flowing like a river, can seem very strange. To those who understand the power of Jesus' blood, this is not only familiar, but also comforting. The prophet Ezekiel paints a beautiful picture of the Mighty River of God.[2] It originates in the Holy of Holies and flows from under the threshold of the Temple. In this illustration, the river begins small but soon becomes a mighty rushing force. Healing and life ebb and flow with every ripple of the living waters.

Ezekiel 47:1 Afterward he brought me again unto the door of the house; and, behold, waters issued out from under the threshold of the house eastward: for the forefront of the house stood toward the east, and the waters came down from under from the right side of the house, at the south side of the altar. KJV

Isaiah 28:16 Therefore thus saith the Lord GOD, Behold, I lay in Zion for a foundation a stone, a tried stone, a precious corner stone, a sure foundation: he that believeth shall not make haste. KJV

Ephesians 2:20 And are built upon the foundation of the apostles and prophets, Jesus Christ himself being the chief corner stone; KJV

It is through Jesus our threshold, that we enter into the house of God and come under the protection of God's roof. It is also through Jesus, the source of the River of Life, that deliverance and healing flow.

One day, in the West African country of Benin, I was speaking about forgiveness. At the end of the service, I invited people to come to the front for prayer. I told them that if anyone needed special prayer, that the pastor or I would pray for them. I suggested that perhaps there were those in the group who were holding unforgiveness toward someone and needed to confess that verbally. An old woman came up and began to speak to the pastor. I watched as the woman animatedly shared her heart. After the pastor prayed for her, she returned to her seat. The pastor then came upfront to sit by me.

A few moments later a young woman came crawling on her hands and knees. She crawled right up to the same old woman who had just spent time in prayer with the pastor. Laying her head on the elder woman's lap she wept and cried. The pastor turned to me and told me to watch as the drama unfolded before us. Then he too began to cry. "Do you see what is happening," he asked me? Then he began to describe how the two women had been estranged for several years, how the old woman had just confessed her unforgiveness towards her daughter, and how she wanted the young woman to come home. The daughter, who had no idea of her mother's prayers, had been sitting outside of the church. Longing to be reconciled with her mother, she had humbled herself by crawling into the church, hoping for forgiveness. I had just shared about the power of forgiveness and before my eyes this drama had unfolded. There in the midst of the church, the River of Life flowed down the aisles, and right into the hearts of two who desperately needed to drink of its healing power.

Jesus told the story of a father and son in the Gospel of Luke.[3] Having just received his inheritance, the son left his father and his home. Thinking his fortune would never end, the young man thoughtlessly and foolishly spent it all. Hard times came, and unemployment was at an all-time high. The only job the young man could get was feeding pigs, and the only food he found to eat was their leftovers. For a young Israelite this was as low as he could go. Pigs were considered to be unclean, and it was forbidden, by the Law of Moses, to even touch them, to say nothing about eating after them.[4] Repulsed by his situation, and desperately hungry, he began to think about all he had left behind. He remembered his father and recalled how well even the hired help were treated. "I'm going home," he said to himself. "Maybe if I beg forgiveness and admit that I have been a fool, my father will at least allow me to work for him. His servants are better off than I am."

Never dreaming that his father would ever allow him to return to his former place as a son, the young man started

> ***There in the midst of the church, the River of Life flowed down the aisles, and right into the hearts of two who desperately needed to drink of its healing power.***

home. There must have been many voices speaking to him as he traveled the long weary journey. "Don't go back. They don't want you there. Everyone has forgotten you. Forgive you? No, not after how foolish you have been." Voices of fear and defeat must have walked alongside of him whispering, "Run the other way. It's hopeless. No one loves you any more." Yet on and on he went never giving up.

The young man's father began to cry as, in the distance, he saw his beloved son walking towards home. Since the young man had left, the father had taken every opportunity to look far in the distance, hoping to see his boy return. As soon as he saw his son the excited father jumped to his feet and began to shout orders. "Everyone listen to me. Quickly go and get the fatted calf." Shouting, he continued, "Go get all the special things that I have set aside just for this day. Hurry! He is almost here. I want everything ready, as soon as he arrives."

Unable to contain his excitement any longer, the old man ran down the road to greet his son. "You're home! You're home! Praise be to God, you're home," sobbing he embraced his son.[5] Supplied with a beautiful robe, new shoes, and a ring, the young man walked to the house with his father's hand tightly entwined in his. The fatted calf was prepared for sacrifice just as they arrived.[6] The son recognized the significance of what was happening as the blood of the Covenant flowed. Weeping, he whispered to his father, "I'm sorry. I'm so sorry. I'm not worthy to be your son. Please let me work for you."

Before the young man could say any more, the father stopped him exclaiming, "We will speak of this no more. You are my son. Today you have come home and it's time to celebrate."

This story, with all of its significant elements, symbolizes the grace that is ours when we return to God and come into right Covenant relationship with him. The robe represents our robe of righteousness; the ring symbolizes ownership and authority that is ours in Christ. The "fatted calf" was the animal prepared for sacrifice, most likely killed in the doorway of the home, offering the blood of the Covenant, that mighty river of God, which flows with love, forgiveness, and friendship.

Like the old mother in Benin and the father of the lost son, our heavenly Father longs for us to come home. He patiently waits for us in eager anticipation of our arrival. The river of God flowing with forgiveness and healing is available for all who come and drink from that living water. The blood flows not only for those who come to the doorway of God's house for the first time but also for those who return after walking away from God. If you find yourself walking the long road home, never give up. Keep on walking. The road home is full of road signs that say, "Turn around and run the other way." Don't give in to the voices of discouragement and despair. Never give up. The Father is waiting for you.

This story, with all of its significant elements, symbolizes the grace that is ours when we return to God and come into right Covenant relationship with him.

Chapter 5
The Hand of Might

I was praying for some people at the church altar, one Sunday, when a woman came to me with an unusual request. "Please, would you pray for a little dog I just saw on my way to church," she asked. "He was laying on the side of the road, and he looked like he had been badly hurt."

I thought, "Why not! Isn't God big enough to care about even the smallest of problems?"

> **Luke 12:6-7** Are not five sparrows sold for two pennies? And not one of them is forgotten before God. Why, even the hairs of your head are all numbered. Fear not; you are of more value than many sparrows. RSV

When I was a little girl, someone told me that I shouldn't bother God with my small problems. That person continued to say that God was so busy with the big issues of life, that He didn't have time for my little "unimportant" things. Thinking this was true, I felt sorry for God and I couldn't even begin to imagine dealing with all the great troubles of the world. After I grew up, I discovered that God is not only big enough to care for all of the world's problems, but to also tend to the smallest details of life. I also discovered that we honor God when we believe in the greatness of His ability, to not only care about wars, earthquakes, and famines, but that He also cares about our small details.

Niagara Falls, Ontario, Canada had advertised a fabulous Christmas light display. Ontario wasn't to far from our home, in Pennsylvania, so Fred, our son, and I planned a trip. We started off early; so that we could do some Christmas shopping before it was dark enough to best enjoy the lights. We promptly filled our car with many Christmas treasures.

Later, after it was dark, we drove around the area looking at all of the beautiful lights. As we were enjoying the lights, I saw a sign that said, "Free Poinsettia Show". That seemed like a fun and festive thing to do, so Fred parked the car, and off we went in search of Christmas flowers, and also more lights.

I also discovered that we honor God when we believe in the greatness of His ability, to not only care about wars, earthquakes, and famines, but that He also cares about our small details.

After we walked past, what seemed like hundreds of flower and light displays, Fred said, "Why don't you stay here? I'll walk back to the car and drive back to pick you up. It won't take me long." This seemed like a great idea, however Fred did not return as quickly as we thought he would.

When Fred arrived at the car he found glass everywhere. Someone had broken the front passenger window and, of all things, stolen my large craft bag. Now this bag held nothing of great value. Inside were my hairbrush, some Christmas candy and gum, a few pens, Kleenex, coins, a greeting card and a cross-stitch project I had been working on. The thief had chosen to take my bag and nothing else. He had missed all the newly purchased Christmas gifts and other valuables we had locked in the car.

Fred picked us up and we went to the Ontario police station to report the theft and damage. Shaking his head the policeman kindly said, "I'm very sorry. You will probably never see your bag again." I was very sad and also a little confused. Why did the thief take my bag, and only my bag, when the car was full of wonderful things that we had just purchased?

We now had to travel back to our home with a broken passenger window. Traveling through New York State on snowy wind blown roads added to my frustration. I was more than just a little upset. Feeling anger and disappointment, I felt sad all the way home. I couldn't help wondering why the thief took my things. He didn't touch anything else. I was frustrated and also a little ashamed for being so upset about my small things. After awhile, Fred finally said, "Don't worry. I'll buy you a new bag."

As kind as Fred's offer had been, nothing would make me feel better. I just wanted my bag back. I didn't like the idea that something had been stolen from me. "It isn't right. It just isn't right," I lamented over and over. I decided I had better pray about this because I was quickly losing my peace.

The only answer I received from God was, "Trust Me."

Six months later, on a Monday morning, I received a phone call from the Ontario police. They wanted to know if I was certain that my bag had been stolen. I assured them that it had been and reminded them that Fred and I had even filled out a theft report in their station, detailing the loss of the bag, and the broken car window. I then asked them why they wanted to know. They said that just the day before, the bag had been found in a front pew of a local Ontario church. I had never been to that church and we all questioned why the bag had so mysteriously showed up. Nevertheless they said I could come and get it.

God loves us enough to take care of the small stuff as well as the big.

The next week, Fred drove to Canada and got my bag. Inside of it were all of my treasured things, my hairbrush, the Christmas candy and gum, my pens, Kleenex, the greeting card and cross-stitch project, nothing was missing, even all the coins were still there. As I was looking through my bag, God began to speak to my heart. He said, "If I can keep your bag in the hands of a thief for six months, how much more can I keep you?" I was struck by the simplicity of His statement. God cared about my small stuff. He cared about my hairbrush.

Luke 12:6-7, quotes Jesus as saying that not one sparrow is forgotten by God. Not only that, but God even counts the hairs on our head. God is so big, and so great, that He has time for our tiniest possessions. Everything under God's roof is under His protecting power. We need to realize that God loves us enough to take care of the small stuff as well as the big.

God showed the Israelites that He could take care of their small stuff too. When Moses commanded the Hebrews to prepare a lamb and put the blood of the lamb upon the door, the Israelites understood that they were preparing for an honored guest.[1] Moses was telling them that The Lord God Almighty, The Great King of Glory, their Deliverer, was coming. They knew they were about to make a powerful Covenant with the Eternal. That night, not only did the death angel pass over their homes, with the blood-splattered doors, but also God Himself stepped over the blood, and into their house, affirming His Covenant with His people. This Covenant relationship was evidenced by the seemingly insignificant fact that, as they fled Egypt, even their shoes did not wear out.[2]

It was a common practice for men to make sacrifices in their doorways preparing a blood Covenant for an important visitor. Building upon a familiar tradition, Moses instructed the Israelites to put blood on the doorposts. The Israelites understood the significance of this act, for in ancient times when a king would die, his son or replacement would take a tour of the land, looking to see who would be loyal to his crown. Running before him, young men would call out, "The King is coming. The King is coming. Make ready for his arrival." People would hurry to prepare their "Fatted calf", the animal saved for just that occasion.

Families would not only slaughter the calf, allowing the blood to flow across the threshold, but also splatter it all around the doorway so that the sacrifice could be seen from a great distance. Customarily, men would use their hands to mark their doorways with blood. This was done because if a king, or man of power, didn't see the evidence of the Covenant blood, he would assume that there was no welcome offered to him. He would then kill everyone in that household, and thus rid the land of all enemies.[3]

The bloody print, placed on the doorpost was known as the "Red Hand".[4] As followers of Christ, we know the "Red Hand" by another name, "Holy Hands". When we see Biblical references like **Psalms 63:4** that tell us to "Lift up Holy Hands", it is telling us to show the sign of our Covenant with God. This symbol, whether stamped on a doorway or performed in an act of worship, was understood to be the Covenant sign between contracting parties and God. It spoke of trust and authority in the God of your Covenant. It was also known as the "Hand of Might".[5] When God declares that He will deliver us with a strong or mighty hand, He is reminding us that He won't forget His Covenant obligations.[6]

> **Hebrews 10:29** Of how much worse punishment, do you suppose, will he be thought worthy who has trampled the Son of God underfoot, counted the blood of the covenant by which he was sanctified a common thing, and insulted the Spirit of grace? RSV

A blood-marked door was a sacred sign of the Covenant and was treated with the utmost respect.[7] Imagine the feeling of insult should a guest step into this sacred blood. This is exactly the issue addressed in **Hebrews 10:29**. Jesus is our Passover lamb and our Covenant sacrifice. This passage is a direct reference to God's Threshold Covenant.[8] To trample underfoot the Son of God is to stomp through the blood of Christ, revealing the utmost scorn, contempt, and the greatest of insults. What degree of punishment could be given to one who rejects this Covenant of Grace? Illustrated in the following story, such a person is worthy of death, if for no other reason, than because he rejected the free gift of life. The only hope for such a one is a restoration of their Covenant.

Drawing deep breaths as he ran, a young boy burst into the tent shouting, "He's coming, he's coming, your elder brother is coming."

Simon smiled as he thought about his older brother. He hadn't seen him in ages and this unexpected visit pleased him. "Go quickly and kill the fatted calf," He commanded. "I want an especially fine feast ready for his arrival." Quickly a calf, the finest in the herd, was brought and Simon stretched the sacrifice's neck across the threshold of his tent. Slicing his victims' neck he let the blood flow. The servants of the household quickly ran to prepare the feast taking the dead animal with them.

However, Jared, the younger brother, was not arriving for a friendly visit. Servants from both brothers' fields had been in a fight. Tempers flared, fists had been thrown, and now a part of Jared's field had been burned. He was not in the mood for a feast. Ignoring the blood on the threshold, he stomped in and out of the tent. Blood dripping from his shoes, he demanded, "Where is Simon? I must see my brother. NOW!"

When God declares that He will deliver us with a strong or mighty hand, He is reminding us that He won't forget His Covenant obligations.

Shock could not adequately describe the look, on Simon's face, when he arrived and saw the blood of his Covenant trampled upon. Angered by such an insult he began to shout, "Who would dare offend me in such a way?" Not realizing the offender was his beloved brother he shouted, "Find the man and kill him, he does not deserve to live."

Realizing how foolish he had been to angrily rush into his

brother's house, Jared looked down and saw the blood clinging to his shoes. Great remorse gripped his heart as he saw Simon's shocked and angry face. "Brother, forgive me. I didn't know about the sacrifice. You know how I get when I am angry, I wasn't thinking. I can't believe that I got upset over such a small thing. I didn't look where I was going. I was so wrong. Please forgive me."

For what seemed like an eternity, Simon stood sternly looking at his brother. The fate of Jared remained unknown as if suspended in mid air. Then, suddenly, a smile broke upon Simon's face and his eyes began to twinkle, "Forgive you, Jared? Yes! I forgive you. Come, now let's eat and together, we shall renew our Covenant."

We have all been guilty of breaking Covenants. Paul said, when writing to the Roman church, that he had a war inside of himself.[9] He talked about the battle between his natural, sinful man, and the Holy nature of God. Paul was disturbed by the seemingly small stuff, i.e. unclean desires, anger, lust, and fear in his life. He recognized that it is the small things in life that often trip us up. It's the small things like anger, backbiting, gossip, and selfishness, which cause us to fail in our Covenants. Most people don't realize that "small things" like, complaining about a friend behind their back, is breaking their Covenant. We have all broken Covenants and trampled under our feet the blood of the Covenant. Insulting the Spirit of Grace, we have stepped out from under the protection of God's roof. Incredibly, God's mercy is always waiting to welcome us back.

> **2 Corinthians 12:20** For I fear that perhaps I may come and find you not what I wish, and that you may find me not what you wish; that perhaps there may be quarreling, jealousy, anger, selfishness, slander, gossip, conceit, and disorder. RSV

God cares about small things. If God Almighty concerns Himself with these little details, how much more, should we consider the power of small things? Must we constantly live in fear of stepping out of God's house? No! Forgiveness is more powerful than any failure. Nevertheless, we should remember that an unrepentant life style of "seemingly" small sins, such as anger, gossip, and lying, can "trip us up" leading us right out of the house.

God's house has no guard to keep people in or out. Entrance is a free gift. It is only our own self-condemnation that keeps us out of God's house. We can step back over the blood at anytime reestablishing our Covenant with God. Come let us make a Covenant together!

We have all broken
Covenants and trampled
under our feet the blood
of the Covenant.
Insulting the Spirit of Grace,
we have stepped out from
under the protection
of God's roof. Incredibly,
God's mercy is always waiting
to welcome us back.

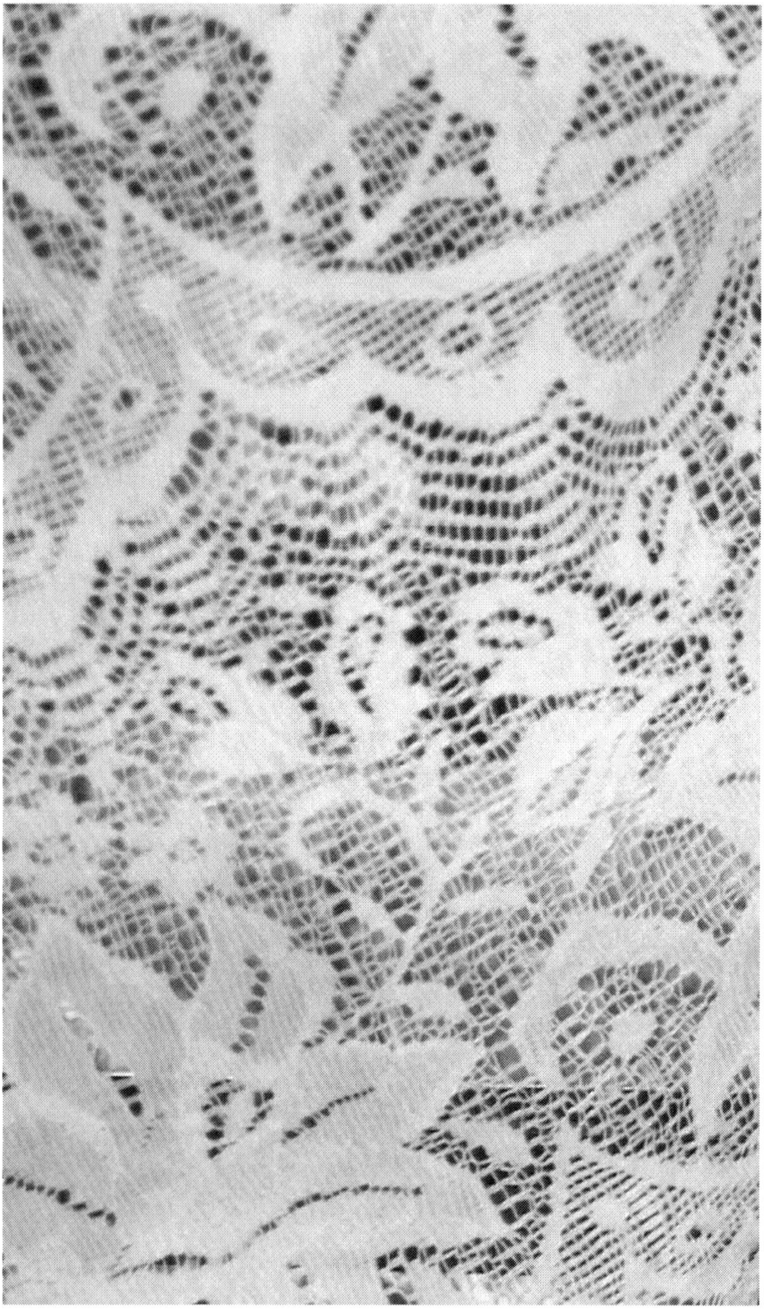

Chapter 6
The Blessed Curse

Twenty men gathered, then it was thirty, fifty, and a hundred. They kept coming, all of them afraid. What should we do? Where can we go? Do we have any choice? Stories of the battle at Jericho had come to every house and the people of Gibeon were terrified. Jericho, with its great walls and mighty army, had been destroyed and conquered. The rumor was that Joshua and his army would soon be at their doorsteps. "We need a plan," someone shouted. "We should fight," said another." "Fight?" came a cry from the back. "We will all be dead. We should just surrender."

"Wait! I have a plan. I know what we should do," an old man said as he hobbled to the front. "The only way out of our situation is in. We have to become one of them. They are a Covenant people. If they Covenant with us, then we will become one of them."

"Make a Covenant?" another man yelled, his fear sounding more like anger. "What kind of nonsense is that? They won't do it! I heard that their God told them to destroy every living soul in the land. What makes you think they will make a Covenant with us?"

The old man sighed, "You are right. They won't want to make a Covenant with us. However we have no choice. We will have to trick them."

So it was decided. Dressed in shabby, worn out clothes, a group of men were sent to see Joshua. In their provisions they carried dried out water bottles and moldy bread. The shoes on their feet were worn and full of holes. Fear pounding in their hearts, they approached Joshua's camp at Gilgal. Would Joshua receive them and more importantly would he believe them or would they all be dead by morning?

Gilgal was a special place near to the oaks of Moreh where Abraham first erected an altar to the Lord.[1] After crossing the Jordan River, Joshua commanded the Israelites to erect 12 stones as a memorial to God at Gilgal. This place was where the Israelites celebrated their first Passover in the new land and renewed their Covenant with God, by circumcising all the males. It was at this place of Covenanting, that the Gibeonites came to see Joshua.

At first, Joshua and the leaders of Israel were skeptical. Were these men truly foreigners or were they really a people who lived close by? Their disguise won out in the end and without consulting the Lord, Joshua, made a Covenant with the people of Gibeon.

It was customary for those wishing to come into a Covenant to abandon all other gods and follow the God of the person they had joined. So it was that the Gibeonites chose to follow the God of Abraham, Isaac, and Jacob. They did this willingly to save their lives. In return, Joshua promised to regard them as one of his own and protect Gibeon at all costs.

Three days later, scouting out the land, Joshua and his men discovered that they had been tricked. The city of Gibeon was only a few miles away. "How could you do such a thing," Joshua demanded of the Gibeonites. The Gibeonites had nothing to lose, so they told the truth. "We heard what your God had done for you," they replied. "We heard about all the battles you had fought and won. We believed that you would soon come to our city and kill us all. We felt we had no choice. You can do what you want with us."

The people in Joshua's camp murmured and complained, "How could you be so stupid Joshua? You didn't even ask God about these people. What kind of a leader are you anyway?"

Joshua responded by reminding them that they had made a Covenant and that there was nothing to be done but to keep it. He then decided that the Gibeonites should be punished and pronounced a curse saying, "From this day forward, you will be responsible for chopping wood and carrying water for the tabernacle."

The Gibeonites soon found that this curse was a blessing in disguise. They were required to dwell in the house of the Lord forever. They were commanded to keep the numerous fires, built for sacrifices, burning. They also had to carry the water for the priests. This water was used to wash the priest's hands as well as the sacrifices. It was hard work indeed, but one that held benefits yet unseen.

Imagine being cursed with responsibility for keeping the fire of God burning? It is difficult to comprehend the awesomeness of this punishment. These people had been given the gift of God's presence, one that had been rejected by so many. In **Exodus 20:18-20,** Moses had asked the children of Israel to go up the mountain, into God's presence, but they refused, wishing for Moses to go up alone. The Apostle Paul tells in **Romans 11:11,** that the Jews failed in their responsibility and therefore made a way into God's house for us. The cry of David's heart was that he would dwell in the house of the Lord forever. The Gibeonites made it into the house of God and went right to the altar of sacrifice, "cursed" to dwell in the house of the Lord forever. Their story doesn't end here, for their cities became Israelite Cities of Refuge and their people were changed from glory to glory. Their curse, a blessing in disguise, made the people of Gibeon an inheritance and from them came prophets, priests and kings.[2]

An inheritance is a legacy or birthright. Therefore, when I think of an inheritance, I think about houses, land, or money. It represents something of great value. I have never heard someone say, "Wow! I just got a five dollar inheritance". On the other hand, I have heard a person rejoice as they tell everyone about their new house, car, or the large bank account they received as an inheritance from someone's estate.

In **Joshua 21:17,** the city of Gibeon and all of its' surrounding lands became an inheritance for Benjamin. The name Benjamin means "Son of The Right Hand", or sitting on the side of blessing and favor. Benjamin was the youngest and,

The Gibeonites soon found that this curse was a blessing in disguise. They were required to dwell in the house of the Lord, forever

after Joseph, the favorite of his father Jacob. An inheritance for the favorite would be the best. In light of this, if the property of Gibeon became the inheritance for Benjamin, what does this tell us about the people of Gibeon? It means they have become something of great value. At one time the Gibeonites had been marked for death. They expected to be destroyed, but instead were brought out of bondage, and now they are a choice treasure chosen for the favored son.

Deuteronomy 4:20 says that we have been brought out of bondage to become the Lord's inheritance. Do you ever feel like you are a "nobody", that you have no value? You really are special. As a matter of fact, God sees you as His treasured possession. Peter says, in **1 Peter 2:9**, that you are a chosen race, a royal priesthood, a holy nation, and God's own people. You were chosen, picked out from all the rest as the best choice. God has not provided Himself with a second-class, good-for-nothing inheritance. He chose you as His portion and His treasure!

> **Psalms 33:12** Blessed is the nation whose God is the LORD; and the people whom he has chosen for his own inheritance. KJV

As parents, we all want the best for our children. When my son was in his mid-twenties he began looking for a wife. One day I asked him about a certain young woman. He told me that she was so wonderful that he would never be able to measure up to her. She was the best and, according to him, would not be interested in "him". I heard, "The best!"

Immediately, in my heart, I decided she was the one for him. Only the best was good enough for my son. Less than a year later, she was his wife! God wants the best for us. He chose us to be His own inheritance and only the best will be sufficient.

One of my desires in writing about Covenant is not to expose broken Covenants and reveal curses, but instead to bring people into an awareness of the blessings that are theirs if they uphold their Covenants. Jesus said in **Matthew 5:13-16**, that we are the Salt of the earth. He was speaking to us in a Covenant Language. He was literally saying you are God's representative of Covenant. If you do not keep your Covenants, what value do you have? Jesus goes on to say that we are the light of the world and compares us to a city set upon a hill. He used this illustration to show us that our lives cannot be concealed, but are revealed for all to see.[3] If we keep our Covenants, God will bless us and we will shine like the sun, and the sin we have hidden in the darkness, will be destroyed as it is exposed to the light.

Once they came, committing themselves in Covenant to Almighty God, their whole lives changed.

In 1629, John Winthrop, the soon to be mayor of the Massachusetts Bay Colony, delivered a speech while sailing to the new world.[4] His speech was called, "We Shall Be As A City Upon A Hill." In the speech he says, "Thus stands the case between God and us. We are entered into a Covenant with him for this work. We have taken out a commission." He goes on to say that because of this Covenant they had made with God, if they kept their part of the Covenant, they would be blessed. However if they did not, they would be cursed. He said that the only way to avoid disaster is to do as the prophet Micah had said. Micah told them to walk humbly with God, to love mercy and to be just, in essence to keep their Covenant with God. In doing this, they would be completely and overwhelmingly blessed. Winthrop wanted his people to know that the whole world would be watching their success or failure.

> **Micah 6:8** He has showed you, O man, what is good; and what does the LORD require of you but to do justice, and to love kindness, and to walk humbly with your God? RSV

Winthrop wanted New England to be blessed, but more than that, he wanted the new land to become an inheritance for future generations. Many of the people who had come to America had been rejected and unwanted in other countries. These people came looking for a new life. Like the Gibeonites, they had no other hope. Once they came, committing themselves in Covenant to Almighty God, their whole lives changed. They not only found a new life for themselves and their children, but also helped found the America we enjoy today. New England not only received an inheritance, they became an inheritance for others.

When we first arrived in Africa, our friend, Pastor Paul introduced us to Susanne. He told us her remarkable story. Years ago, Susanne noticed that one by one her family had been dying. It seemed that there was no one left but she and her sister. Her family had been animists and worshiped demons. Susanne realized that her sister was serious about her demonic worship. Her sister's demonic spirits demanded a regular human sacrifice year after year and as a result she had been cursing her family members until, mysteriously, all had died except for Susanne. Our new friend knew she would be the next victim. In great fear, she began to seek out an answer to her predicament. She had heard about Pastor Paul and knew that he was a man of God. She came to him telling of her fears. He told her that the only way to be safe was through the blood of Jesus. Basically what he said was, "The only way out is in." She had to come into the kingdom of God, enter his house, exchanging her life for Jesus' and she would be saved. Quickly Susanne accepted the Lord Jesus and her life was spared.

Like the Gibeonites, Susanne had been destined for death. She had no hope and no future. Coming to God and making a life exchange with Him changed her future and today Susanne has a good job and a wonderful family. She is an active Christian and church member. God has blessed her in many ways and she gives Him all the glory.

Many people in Africa have told me similar stories. The only way to be safe from demonic activity is to become adopted into the family of God and live in His house. The only way out of certain death for the Gibeonites was to make a Covenant with Joshua, entering into Israel's household. The Bible says, in **Joshua 11:19**, that the Gibeonites were the only ones who asked for this grace and mercy.

God chose you as the best for Himself. It is grace that makes you acceptable to Him. Perhaps in your own eyes you see yourself as undesirable. However nothing is too good for our loving heavenly Father, and He chose you to be His "City On a Hill" (a demonstration of His love), His own inheritance. He wants you to be blessed as you walk in this Covenant. He wants the entire world to see what He has done for you. Is this hard to believe? Moses said in **Deuteronomy 32:9** that the LORD'S portion is his people. **Psalms 33:12** says that God chooses people for his own inheritance. And **Psalms 94:14** reminds us that the LORD will never forsake us because we are His inheritance.[5]

After Peter explains in **I Peter 2:9**, that we are a royal and chosen generation, he goes on in verse ten to say that where as once we were a "nobody" now, we are a "somebody." Through this marvelous Covenant, we have become someone special, a person of position. It is by grace and not by works that we obtain this favor. Wonderful grace. God has set us apart as His inheritance and he has set us high above all others. Never question the Lord's favor. Never doubt His unending kindness towards you. Never doubt the forgiving power of our Almighty God for, "The Only Way Out Is In!"

He chose you
to be His
"City On a Hill" .
His own inheritance.
He wants you to be
blessed as you
walk in this
Covenant.

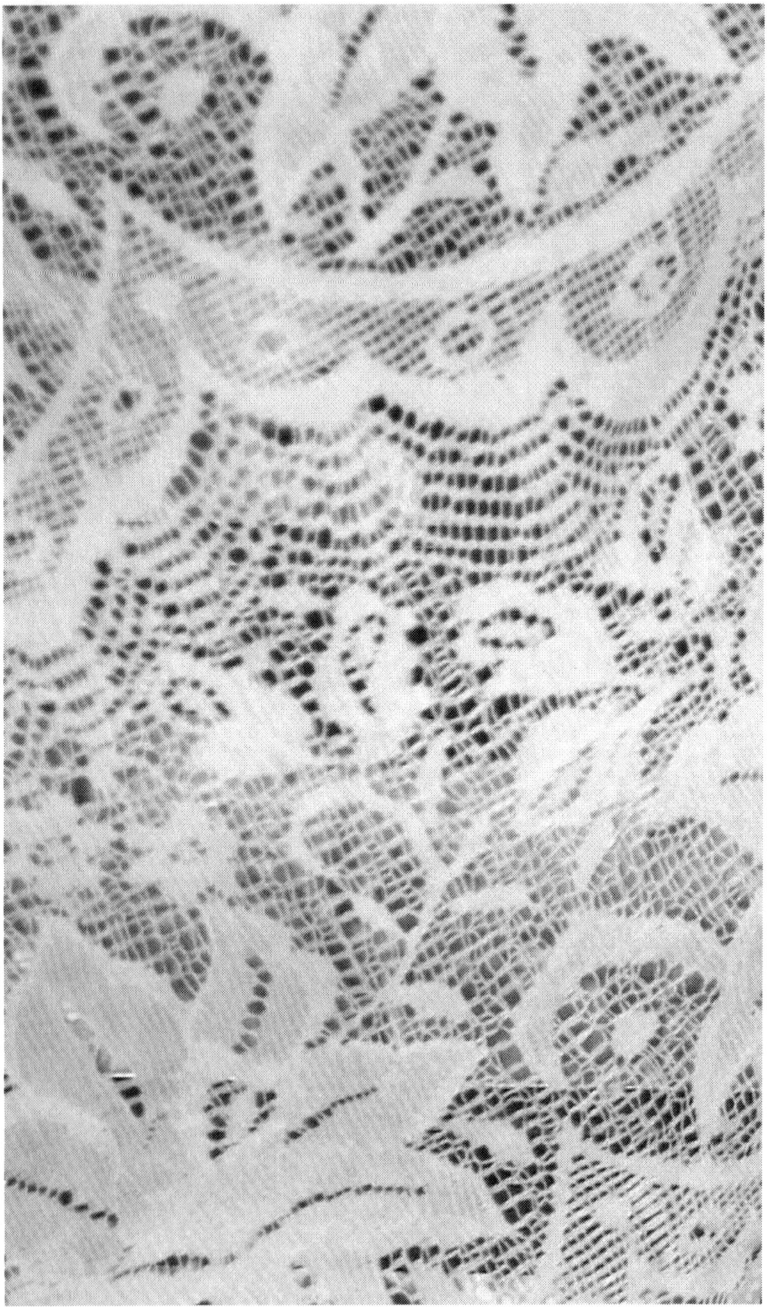

Chapter 7

Stones From Heaven

Psalms 37:40 And the LORD shall help them, and deliver them: he shall deliver them from the wicked, and save them, because they trust in him. KJV

It was a fantastic turn of events. The Gibeonites had always been friendly with their neighbors and had been allies with them for generations. Suddenly, the tables were turned for the Gibeonites had joined forces with Joshua and the Israelites. Five of the most powerful kings in the land conferred and decided betrayal like this had to be stopped. So they surrounded the city of Gibeon. With no one else to turn to, Gibeon sent word to Joshua, "Come and help us."

A three-day scouting trip in the hot dry climate had left Joshua and his men weary. Families, running to greet their loved ones as they neared Gilgal, unexpectedly heard the cry from a runner. "Gibeon, your Covenant friends, have been surrounded by their enemies. You must come quickly and help them."

If I had been Joshua, I may have thought, "Go help Gibeon? They just tricked me. We don't even know these people. My men are tired. If I delay, Gibeon's enemies will destroy them and I will be rid of these lying, deceitful people." Instead, Joshua immediately responded with, "Where are my finest men? We leave at once." Marching all night at their fastest pace, the men retraced their steps back to the city of Gibeon. They had just spent three days on this road but this night, in hast they made the torturous journey by morning. A man of Covenant is marked by how quickly he can forgive. Joshua wasted no time forgiving the people of Gibeon of their deceit and then coming to their aid.

Covenant says, "I will do my Covenant friend no harm. I will protect him at any cost."

The Covenant Gibeon had with Joshua is an illustration of the Covenant we have with Jesus. Gibeon had been destined for death. They had been rejected, and then, by making a Covenant with Joshua, a way was made for them to come into God's house. Joshua came to fight for them and became their, "knight in shining armor" or Covenant Redeemer. We too were rejected and marked for death. We were destined for an eternity separated from God. Then Jesus came, shed his blood for us, and offered us salvation. Like Joshua fulfilling his Covenant with Gibeon, Jesus is our Covenant Redeemer.

Covenant says, "I will do my Covenant friend no harm. I will protect him at any cost." Gibeon's enemies were now

Joshua's enemies. Joshua would have never considered breaking his Covenant, for he understood the consequences. He also knew that, in keeping the Covenant, he was under the protection of God Almighty and that his God would fight for him. Everything he needed was provided for in the Covenant.

As Joshua and his men started to fight, fear filled the hearts of his enemies and they began to run away. Then the Lord caused great hailstones from heaven to fall and more men were killed from the hail than from the swords of Joshua's army. The battle was the Lord's and Israel's supernatural resources were enormous.

All Joshua had to do was show up to the battleground and God began to fight for him. Interestingly, Gibeon didn't have to fight at all. If we will come out from our hiding place and show up to the battlefield, God will do the fighting. In spite of this fact, many of us give up in despair, and never see the victories God has already provided. Depression, fear, and anxiety, cause many like King Saul's soldiers facing Goliath, to miss the experience and thrill of seeing God's miraculous power. The battle is the Lord's, because we have entered into his house, and he is obligated, by the terms of the Covenant, to protect us.

There is an old fable about an elephant and a mouse. The elephant and mouse were traveling together; the mouse perched high behind the right ear of the elephant. As they passed over a bridge, the weight of the elephant caused the bridge to groan and sway. On the other side the mouse exclaimed, "Boy we really shook that bridge, didn't we?" Of course, it wasn't the weight of the mouse that shook the bridge, but he wanted to share credit with the elephant. The same is true for us when we walk with Christ. As we come to the problems of life, Jesus carries us. He is the elephant and we are the mouse. He shakes our problems and we just get carried through them. The battles we face belong to the Lord. He is our defender and protector. Like Joshua was for Gibeon, Jesus is our Covenant Redeemer.

Historians say that this battle was one of the most important battles in ancient world history.[1] The alliance with Gibeon was also a political victory and it strengthened Joshua's authority in the eyes of the surrounding nations. Joshua fought the armies of five of the most powerful kings in the land. As he fought, Joshua secured his hold in the Promised Land. This battle settled the course of events that even affect us today.

Before Joshua went to the aid of Gibeon, God promised that He would be with Joshua and that He would deliver all of Joshua's enemies into his hand. Before we go into any spiritual battle, God has also given us the assurance that He is in control and will give us the victory. We never have to be afraid or worry that God is not with us. His Word promises that He is with us always and that He will never leave us.

> **2 Corinthians 12:9** And He said to me, "My grace is sufficient for you, for My strength is made perfect in weakness." Therefore most gladly I will rather boast in my infirmities, that the power of Christ may rest upon me. NKJV

God said that His grace is sufficient. Grace speaks of favor and of friendship. As Joshua defended his Covenant with Gibeon, God provided grace upon grace, and gave Joshua victory over his enemies. When you become a defender of Covenant, like Joshua, you prepare yourself for some of the greatest victories in your life.

> **Psalms 121:1-2** I will lift up mine eyes unto the hills, from whence cometh my help. My help *cometh* from the LORD, which made heaven and earth. KJV

God was preparing me for a victory one day, as I was running some errands and I drove away from my house. I began to ponder upon a frustrating problem. I was upset but decided that I was not going to allow this troubling situation to control me. I had learned, a long time ago, that the things that we dwell upon have power over us. I was making an effort to think about the Word of God, choosing to take my thoughts captive.

> **2 Corinthians 10:4-5** For the weapons of our warfare *are* not carnal but mighty in God for pulling down strongholds, casting down arguments and every high thing that exalts itself against the knowledge of God, bringing every thought into captivity to the obedience of Christ. NKJV

While I was out, my sister called me on my cell phone. She asked me how I was doing and I told her that I was "pulling down strongholds" (A fortress- anything that someone relies on). She asked me what I meant and I told her that when we take our thoughts captive, it is spiritual warfare and that God begins to fight for us. We then begin to pull down false strongholds and make God our fortress and defender. I intended to control my thoughts so that the battles I was fighting would never come against my children. After we talked for a while, I realized that it was time to go home. So we concluded our conversation and I drove home.

Grace speaks of favor and of friendship. As Joshua defended his Covenant with Gibeon, God provided grace upon grace, and gave Joshua victory over his enemies.

Our driveway goes uphill at a steep slant. In order to go up the drive, I had to completely stop in front of the house, turn the steering wheel sharply, and step on the gas. I did this and pulled into the backyard. Just as I entered the house, I heard an explosion like I had never heard before and a light flashed all through the house. Marie-Louise then told me that just before I had arrived, there had been two other house-shaking explosions.

Joshua didn't look for a reason to give up. He commanded a reason to finish his fight.

I began to look around the house for a fire when another startling BANG occurred, louder than the last. I raced through the house to determine if we were in danger. I looked, through the window on our front door, and saw electric wires from the high voltage electric pole in front of our house. They had somehow frayed and were exploding. The wires were falling on the ground exactly where I had just stopped my car to go up the driveway.

For me, it was like "time stood still". I remembered how I had been actively taking my thoughts captive and how I had been making myself think about how the Lord would help me. Then I recalled how that only moments before, I had stopped the car in the exact spot where hot electrical wires could have fallen on my car or me. I had been where the wires had exploded but I hadn't seen anything unusual. I had driven up to the house right between explosions and God had protected me. I had just declared that the Lord would fight for me and in that very moment He actually did.

Joshua had a moment when "time stood still", while he was fighting for Gibeon. As the enemies of Gibeon were running away, Joshua knew that he needed more time to fight and win a complete victory. He spoke to the sun and the moon commanding them to stand still. Joshua didn't look for a reason to give up. He commanded a reason to finish his fight. The sun and moon obeyed giving Joshua the time to completely destroy his enemies. In **Joshua 10:14** we are told that there had never been a day like this, when the Lord answered such a request from man. God would move heaven and earth to answer Joshua's prayers.

Jesus also spoke to His problem in **Mark 4:39**. He and his disciples were in a boat when a great storm came and the disciples were afraid. Jesus calmly spoke and said, "Peace, be still." The wind and the waves obeyed and the storm was over. Joshua spoke to the sun and it obeyed. Jesus spoke to the storm and it obeyed. We should speak words that change our situation. Many people only use words to describe their circumstances. I spoke to my stormy thoughts and they too obeyed. It's part of our Covenant because we have entered God's house and now our problems belong to Him.

> **Isaiah 65:24** And it shall come to pass, that before they call, I will answer; and while they are yet speaking, I will hear. KJV

Marie-Louise was only six years old when we adopted her. Her lifestyle had an abrupt change. She moved into our house and had her own bedroom. She was used to sleeping on the floor with other children, and was a little afraid. Shortly after she moved into our house, we had a loud thunderstorm. I was sound asleep when I felt Fred stirring. I asked him where he was going and he said, "The storm is getting worse and I think Marie-Louise will be afraid." He crept down the stairs and was almost standing in her doorway just as the loudest clap of thunder rang through the house. Marie-Louise jumped and cried out, "Daddy where are you?" Immediately Fred replied, "I was here even before you called."

Traveling in Africa, I have many opportunities to trust in the Lord. One night in particular, we were traveling with a team to Accra, Ghana, from Cotonou, Benin. The day had so many delays that we ended up traveling in the dark. After some time we were stopped by police looking for trouble. They wanted a bribe and we didn't want to give them one. They told us to unload the minibus we were in. We were a group of ten and this was a lot of luggage to unload in the dark. In the van, we started singing about the "Faithfulness of God". The next thing we knew the police were letting us go. We were stopped several times that night and we continued to sing about the faithfulness of God. When we arrived at the guesthouse, my daughter-in-law asked me to help her open her suitcase. It was stuck and would not open. After struggling with it over and over, she said, "Maybe we should sing our song." So we sang, "We've come this far by faith!" I declared that the God who helped us on the road also had the power to open zippers and suddenly the zipper worked. Now this may seem simple to you but it was definitely the hand of God.

In **Isaiah 65:24,** we are told that God is there for us even before we call Him. God was with me as I drove up my driveway. Fred was in Marie-Louise's doorway before she called. Joshua dropped everything and came as fast as he could, racing to help Gibeon as soon as he heard their call.

Disaster threatens on every corner, yet we are untouched. We have all traveled just moments before or after major car accidents. Disease and natural disasters are all around us, yet we don't have to live our lives afraid. God is with us.

Once again He can cause the sun to stand still. When we make God our fortress and source, in times of trouble, we recognize the significance of His Covenant with us. We have stepped over the blood and entered into an agreement that is unbreakable and unchangeable. Speak to your storms. Your battle will come to an end. I think you will be amazed to see how often the sun will stand still for you.

When we make God our fortress and source, in times of trouble, we recognize the significance of His Covenant with us. We have stepped over the blood and entered into an agreement that is unbreakable and unchangeable.

Chapter 8
The Thief

A lot of young people call me mom. As a result, I often have prayer requests from these "adopted" sons and daughters. One particular young man, Tim, was going through a very difficult trial and, as I was praying for him, I heard God say, "Pray against a Trojan Spirit." A Trojan Spirit? That was the second time I had prayed for someone and the Lord had directed me to pray in this manner.

The first time I heard the Holy Spirit prompt me to pray against a Trojan Spirit was for Will another friend of mine.[1] God told me that a Trojan spirit was responsible for Will's problems. I asked the Lord to protect my young friend from this evil presence. As I prayed, the legendary Trojan horse came to my mind. This story, set during the Trojan War, portrays a giant wooden horse, given by the Greeks to their enemies, the Trojans. The horse was understood to be a peace offering so the Trojans dragged their gift inside the city walls. Later that night, Greek soldiers, hiding inside of the horse's hollow belly, snuck out. From inside the fortress, the hidden soldiers opened the gate. With the help from fellow soldiers outside, the Greeks captured the city of Troy. I assumed a Trojan spirit was sneaky, like the historical horse, and was able to gain access to someone through trickery.

Will was sick and seemed unable to get well. He had also made a casual friendship with someone of questionable character. This new friend brought many costly gifts and much confusion, suggesting "seemingly" innocent doubts and questions. I felt compelled, by the Holy Spirit, to direct Will to throw away anything he had received from his new friend. Having traveled extensively in Africa and Asia, I knew that spirits often attach themselves to objects. I did not want Will to unknowingly keep something that might have spiritual "strings attached". He did what I asked, and quickly regained his health.

Simple statements readily received in fertile hearts, became like a Trojan horse filled with enemy soldiers, ready to attack and destroy. Because of the influence of a Trojan spirit both Tim and Will doubted who they were in Christ. They both lost their joy and questioned the power and life that the blood of Christ provided them. Becoming entangled with a curse, the spirit began sucking life out of them. They forgot the authority that was theirs because of the Blood of Jesus, their Covenant Redeemer. Both were given many gifts with "strings attached". The gifts in themselves were benign, however they had a subtle evil authority attached to them. It was as if the gifts were given to buy not only loyalty, but also their souls. Receiving gifts from a Trojan spirit pretends a pseudo-Covenant, bringing bondage and even death. These gifts, like the mythical Trojan horse containing unseen power, needed to be removed from their lives. Without intervention, both young men could have gone down a path far away from their Covenant destiny.

> **John 10:1** Truly, truly, I say to you, He that enters not by the door into the sheepfold, but climbs up some other way, the same is a thief and a robber. RSV

Simple statements readily received in fertile hearts, became like a Trojan horse filled with enemy soldiers, ready to attack and destroy.

Remember, Jesus said that a thief would not enter a house through the door, but that he would enter in another way, most likely through a back entrance, window, or even digging underneath. In the case of a Trojan, the thief enters by trickery or deceit.[2] From our study we know that the door was the place of Covenant. In history, there are many tales of thieves, who even though having the heart to steal, would honor the Covenant if he stepped through the gate or over a person's threshold.[3] It is for this reason that, in many cultures, it was unnecessary to put a guard at the front of a house. The only way the thief could steal was to enter another way. Likewise, the Trojan spirit comes another way and is a thief.

Today there is a new application for the name, Trojan horse. A Trojan horse is a destructive computer program that masquerades as a benign application. At first glance it appears to be a good and helpful program, but will actually do damage to your computer. Unlike computer viruses, Trojan horses do not reproduce themselves, but they can be just as destructive. Not only can they do great damage, but they also have the power to create a back door into your computer system. This would allow future access by unknown persons to your computer and it's files.

Just like the computer version, a Trojan horse spirit can come into our lives as something innocent, allowing future access and destruction. Once, when Fred and I were visiting some friends in Africa, I observed their young daughter, as she watched cartoons and Sci-Fi shows on the television. This family happened to be blessed with Cable TV, which was becoming more and more popular in that part of Africa. Fred and I had always been very careful what we watched on TV and I was shocked to see what was available on the televisions in Africa. Every day, the little eight-year old would watch cartoons showing demons and devils doing sorcery and violence.

One day, I mentioned my concern to her father and he just thought I was having a problem with legalism. I argued with him that I wasn't legalistic. I didn't have a problem watching television. I just didn't think a small child should be watching such demonic stuff. He basically shrugged his shoulders and walked away from me, allowing the child to resume her afternoon cartoon ritual. His response seemed very unusual to me, because Africans know and understand the power of curses and witchcraft.

That night as I was sleeping in their house, I felt someone or something touch me on the shoulder. I woke up to see the same creature, from the demonic cartoon, leering at me. He was laughing as if to say, "I won." He was, I believe, a Trojan spirit who had entered the house as an innocent cartoon. Now he had permission to live in the house.

Anything that sneaks into your life and steals your joy and takes your Covenant blessing is a Trojan Spirit.

It wasn't long before we began to see problems multiply in our friend's house. A spirit of sickness came in. For several months the mother was unwell and no one could find the cause. For no apparent reason, the husband lost many of his oldest and dearest friends. Even today, years later, I continue to hear stories about this family that make me feel sad. Unfortunately, this story does not have a happy ending. The Trojan horse seemed to have found himself a home.

Anything that sneaks into your life and steals your joy and takes your Covenant blessing is a Trojan Spirit. It does not come through your front door but like the computer program, comes through a back entrance. Paul talked about this in the book of Galatians. He asks the Galatians, "Who has tricked you?"[4] Someone has come into your life, tricked you into believing another message and took your blessing. Paul tells them that they don't have to settle for a curse. Jesus became a curse for us and now the curse does not have permission to be a part of our lives. Paul goes on to say that if a curse is given a home, it will stay. And those who receive the curse will then be subjected to the laws and regulations of that curse.

> **Galatians 3:13** Christ redeemed us from the curse of the law, having become a curse for us. RSV

There are many fooled by these subtle Trojan spirits. Even the mighty are fallen by Trojans who have snuck into their lives, waiting for the best time to attack. Years ago, Fred and I knew a young couple who had graduated from Bible College. We knew this couple very well and because they were very friendly, everyone liked them. Nevertheless they entertained a Trojan spirit of criticism. They began to criticize many things, including their pastor and their friends. Often offended by seeming injustices they moved repeatedly and had a hard time staying with a job. This should have been a clue that something wasn't right. At one time in their life they were asked to pastor a small country church. At first it seemed like they could do no wrong. However, it wasn't long before the Trojan spirit, with his hidden agenda was exposed. The young pastor was friendly with young girls in the church and they loved his attentions. The pastor was deceived by the Trojan and convinced himself that he was doing no wrong. One day he crossed the lines of propriety, and his actions towards the girls was no longer appropriate. The church quickly dismissed the couple from their position. They ran away to hide, having been attacked and almost destroyed by a Trojan spirit.

> **Zechariah 8:13** And it shall come to pass That just as you were a curse among the nations... So I will save you, and you shall be a blessing. Do not fear, Let your hands be strong. NKJV

Maybe you have allowed a Trojan Spirit to come into your life. The prophet Zechariah tells us that once we were a curse but now we are a blessing. Have hope my dear friend. If the enemy has tricked you, if you have played too long with sin, there is hope for you. You may have been cursed, but God wants you blessed and freed from these tormenting spirits.

Trojan spirits are outside of our Covenant with God. Critical and quick to judge, they act out of the works of the Law. If you find yourself in the camp of the critical, examine your heart. Look at the friends with whom you surround yourself. What kind of people are they? Paul said, in **Galatians 4:24-31**, that bondage

If the enemy has tricked you, if you have played too long with sin, there is hope for you. You may have been cursed, but God wants you blessed.

must go. There are relationships from which we have to separate ourselves, because they represent the Covenant of death. Trojans want to steal from us and watch for our reaction. They want to expose our sin and condemn us, as the Law says we should be condemned. The Apostle Paul often encouraged believers, by telling them that the Law no longer had authority over them. He told them they were given the free gift of grace.[5]

We all have times when our faith is tried. When a Trojan spirit comes knocking on your door, he comes wanting to test your faith. Jesus told Peter that He had prayed for Peter so that his faith would not fail. Jesus never said He would stop the trial. He said He would pray for Peter. He has also prayed for us. Often we enter these times rebuking the devil and feeling stressed beyond measure. Yet these are the times that prove our faith and without them our faith is never strong or increased. Seasons of testing come to enlarge us and increase our faith. Did Peter deny Christ? Yes, but in the end his faith did not fail him. He remained faithful to the Lord and brought thousands to Christ. He died the death of a martyr for the cause of Christ, his faith having never failed. The devil wishes to discourage us all and make us quit. Only those who listen to the voice of the Trojan spirit give up, often moments just before victory.

My friend, George (another young pastor who calls me mom) came to me and said he was having trouble communicating with his wife. They were newly married and sometimes had differences that upset both of them. Distressed he asked, "How do I pray in this situation?" I told him that he should pray like Jesus, that their faith would not fail.

This seemed strange to him until I explained that when you

say marriage vows, you actually declare your faith. You say things like, “For better for worse, in sickness and in health, richer or poorer, I pledge you my faith”. In each situation the vows may differ, yet the Covenant remains the same. When a couple marries, they promise their faith. Faith is the substance, or thing, that cannot be seen, but is promised for a future date.[6] It is only after we have suffered disagreements, trials, persecutions, and misunderstandings, remaining true to our declaration of love, that our faith is proven. To be valid, faith must be proven through trials. Couples, who have endured raising children with all their sicknesses, bumps and bruises, financial struggles, and the fading of physical beauty, can say they have proven their faith. It is on the wedding day that we look ahead to the future and symbolically say, “I see tomorrow and I give you a declaration of my faith, no matter what comes our way, we will still be together. Future trials will only serve to prove (my faith) to you, that what I am promising today is true.”

> **Psalms 23:3** He restores my soul; He leads me in the paths of righteousness For His name's sake. NKJV

When our faith fails it causes soul-sickness. We know that King David suffered from soul-sickness because he said that God restored his soul. Meaning, his soul was healed or brought back to health. Soul-sickness is the most cruel and difficult to endure. It is a sickness brought about by Trojan spirit’s bearing “gifts” of heart-stopping worry, anxiety and stress. It causes one to wonder, “Where is God in my life?” David knew his soul needed to be restored. Many have thought that having our soul restored is salvation but that cannot be true since David, who clearly walked with God, needed his soul restored. He needed a soul-ution. (Pardon the misspelling and pun) The word solution means, the ending of something, breaking, or separation of something. We need to reject the Trojan spirit and kick him out of our house. Our soul needs to be separated from the world, our own devices, and thoughts, in order to be bound to the mind and purposes of Christ. Only then is our soul restored.

Many years ago, when I heard the news that I had cancer, Trojan spirits with their "gifts" of self-pity, attacked my mind using the deepest, darkest, thoughts imaginable. I could not talk or even get out of bed. I was soul-sick. It was then that God spoke to me. He said, "Will you go too?" I knew Jesus was asking me the same question that He had asked Peter many centuries before. Many of Jesus' disciples had become offended with Jesus and, as a result, many disciples had left Him. Jesus then said to Peter, the same words he had just said to me, "Will you go too?"

Our soul needs to be separated from the world, our own devices, and thoughts, in order to be bound to the mind and purposes of Christ. Only then is our soul restored.

I responded, "No Lord, even if I die, I will not go because you are my life." It was then he said to me something I will never forget. "Faith is not faith until it has been tried. It has not been tried until it has been offended. After it has been offended, if it still believes, then it is truly faith. Today you have faith." When I spoke in faith, I shut the door of my heart to the Trojan spirit. Instead of a Covenant of death, I chose a Covenant of Life.

Jesus prayed that Peter's faith would not fail. We too, should pray for those who are going through difficult situations; that their faith would not fail. The trying of their faith becomes their soul-ution. They become stronger, healed, enlarged, and anointed. Peter soon realized that anything worth living for was worth dying for. Anything worth dying for was worth enduring the cross for, the dying to self, the **solution**. It was worth the trying of His faith.

Tim, the young man from the beginning of this chapter, told me that he is very thankful that his faith was tried. It wasn't easy, as a matter of fact, it was one of the hardest times of his life. Today he is stronger and full of faith. During his troubles, he found faith and victory in God, which was his soul-ution. The "trying of his faith" made him strong as he chose to persevere through his problems and trust in the Lord.

Winston Churchill once said, *"...never give in, never give in, never, never, never, never—in nothing, great or small, large or petty—never give in except to convictions of honour and good sense. Never yield to force; never yield to the apparently overwhelming might of the enemy."*[7] He said this when faced with unbelievable odds. The Second World War had come to his shores and all looked bleak. I am sure there were many times he was *soul-sick*. Churchill chose to never give up. He chose instead to believe that right would win and in the end, it did. How about you? Don't give up with the victory within your grasp? Don't allow a Trojan spirit to enter your house, to steal your faith, your joy, and your victory. When you give up, you make a Covenant with death and give an invitation to a Trojan spirit. Shut the door in the face of this spirit and never give in. Never, never, never, never give in!

Chapter 9

Squatter's Rights

There is an old Chinese proverb that says, "*You cannot prevent the birds of sorrow from flying over your head, but you can prevent them from building nests in your hair.*" This proverb addresses both sorrow and squatter's rights. We could substitute any number of problems, feelings, or emotions for the birds of sorrow, but what about squatter's rights?

By definition, squatters are people who live on someone else's land without permission. After they have lived on and taken care of the land for a number of years, they have legal rights to that land. In the United Kingdom, once a squatter lives on the land for a period of ten years or more, they can register the land as theirs.[1] The Land Registry will inform the original owner of this new registration, however, he only has sixty-five days to refute the squatter's claim. He then only has two years to remove the offending squatter. If he fails to do so, the squatter may file for ownership again. In the United States this is called Adverse Possession. Which simply means to take someone's property, occupying it, and claiming ownership, because of the owner's neglect or without his permission. After some years, the person or persons who squat, acquire rights to the property.

Resisting is a lifetime event that requires diligence and tenacity on our part. We must resolve ourselves to this activity.

In the Philippines, if you buy land and there are squatters living on the land, you may have to pay them to leave or compensate them in some way. Some people have gone so far as to say that the squatters have more rights than the landowners. For example, a woman in the Philippines bought some land and when she went to investigate her property she found that thirty or more squatters were living there. She asked for advice and everyone told her that it would be difficult for her to get rid of these squatters. She would daily have to work at removing them. Even if the squatters left today, they could come back tomorrow, and return again the next day, and again the next. She was advised to quickly put up a wall and begin building her house or she would never be rid of the squatters. As a matter of fact, she was warned that if she delayed, the squatters could multiply.

> **Ephesians 2:22** ...In whom you also are built into it for a dwelling place of God in the Spirit. RSV

What does all this have to do with my life you may ask? We have established that we have a home in Christ, and He has His home in us. Ownership of a home demands accountability and responsibility. We have a legal responsibility to keep our home free from harmful things. If we invite a guest to our house, we are obligated to keep our home safe for not only ourselves but also for our invited guest. God is responsible for keeping His home safe and pure for us, His invited guest. We are also responsible for keeping a clean and secure house. Having said that, the last thing we want to do is to allow squatters to come into our life and make their home in us, messing up our place. Like the proverbial birds, squatters pass by our home and even try to visit. We cannot prevent them from passing, but we can stop them from making a nest in our house.

Similar to this woman in the Philippines, we must be diligent in fighting squatters. Squatting spirits would like to come and rest on our land and in our spiritual homes. The Bible says that we should resist the devil and that he would flee from us.[2] This is not a "one time fix-all." Resisting is a lifetime event that requires diligence and tenacity on our part. We must resolve ourselves to this activity. Building walls of protection, we keep the squatters out. Memorizing scripture, taking every thought captive, building our faith by recalling past victories, we fill in the empty spaces where these demonic spirits lived. If we don't, this persistent enemy will return and even bring his friends.[3]

We have established that we have a home in Christ, and He has His home in us. Ownership of a home demands accountability and responsibility. We have a legal responsibility to keep our home free from harmful things.

Proverbs 25:28 Whoever has no rule over his own spirit Is like a city broken down, without walls. NKJV

Jesus, visiting the Temple in Jerusalem, discovered that squatters had invaded the house of God.[4] Moneychangers gradually came in and took over the entrance of the temple. They were squatters and no one hated the squatters enough to get rid of them. Many people actually made a profit from these disreputable merchants and accepted their presence. Under the appearance of devotion to God, wicked men came into the temple and made a mockery of the sacrifices. They pretended ownership of the temple and went so far as to build little shops inside the entrance. Historians indicate that this was not the first time that Jesus drove these people out.[5] In His absence, they had returned. Jesus took ownership of His house and said, “My house shall be called a house of prayer, but you have made it a home of thieves.” He called the temple His house. Jesus then tipped over the tables and booths of these wicked men, chasing them out.

We are the temples of the living God. Jesus speaks over our houses even today and says, “My house shall be a house of prayer, a place of communion (spiritual union or Covenant) with God.”

We are the temples of the living God. Jesus speaks over our houses even today and says, “My house shall be a house of prayer, a place of communion (spiritual union or Covenant) with God.” We need to be like Jesus and hate the thieving squatters enough to fight them. The only rights these spirits have are by default. Many of us have laid down our authority and allowed generational curses, depression, and thoughts of hopelessness to live within us unchallenged. Squatters hope we will let our guard down so that they can sneak inside of our house. Coming in “another way”, they pretend a Covenant with us and demand our respect. They even go so far as to declare themselves the ruler of our spiritual house, claiming rights they don't have. After a while, even the owner of the house no longer knows who is in control.

Many people have had squatting spirits for so long that they think the squatter actually owns the house and has a right to live there. This parasite becomes so familiar with his host that he is no longer noticed. Outsiders can't tell the squatter from the owner. The rightful owner of the house even forgets that the squatter is there, allowing him to whisper thoughts that would persuade those who listen, to give up, become discouraged and perhaps even die. In reality they are usurping thieves who steal hope and every aspect of life.

Once, while my son was attending Bible school, he came into his dorm room while his roommate was making strange faces in the mirror. My son asked his friend what he was doing and he replied, "I am casting a demon out of myself." As strange or funny as this may seem, this is exactly what must be done with squatters. They are in fact demons who want to live in your house and you are the only one who can cast them out. If you don't take authority over them they will not go, as a matter of fact, they will eventually bring their whole family and friends "of like spirit" to camp out in your life.

A Squatting Spirit is different from a Trojan Spirit. A Trojan is invited. He has permission to gain entrance. A Squatter comes uninvited, and because of neglect or an inability to make him leave, he stays. Where as we may invite a spirit of criticism and anger, and even nurse it along, spirits of depression and sorrow are often squatters. I know of many people who suffer from depression and sadness. Not one of them has invited these sad and

Like the birds that fly over our heads, these squatters come, and because our attention is elsewhere, they take up residence. The fault in this situation is not that they are there, but that they are allowed to stay.

depressed spirits into their life. As a matter of fact, these spirits are often told to leave. Tenacious, they hang around until the person finally gives up fighting and just lets the offending spirit stay. Trojans and Squatters are also different in the way that they are dealt with; a Trojan spirit is easily cast out. Once his trickery is discovered you command him to leave and he leaves. The squatter thinks he has rights and refuses to leave or if he does leave, he comes right back. Squatters and Trojans often travel together. For example, a person can become legitimately angry. The word of God says to be angry and sin not.[6] That means there is a right way to be angry. However anger can come like a Trojan, masquerading as a just cause, only to gain access into a life. Trojans open doors and invite Squatters of bitterness and resentment inside the gates of one's spirit. These squatters, like modern day terrorist sleeper cells, take up residence in the name of "righteous indignation", until they have established a firm hold on the person and live like they own the place. Like Jesus said, "These come out only by prayer and fasting." You must have dogged determination.

God, after creating the earth, named the night and the day.[7] In doing so he took ownership of the earth. In the ancient world, if a king named something or someone, he was claiming his dominion over them. Because of sin, the devil became a squatter, who through deception, declared his ownership. In Genesis 26 we see the story of Isaac, the son of Abraham. Because of a famine, he was forced to leave his father's land. During the many years of his absence, Philistine enemies stopped up the wells that Abraham had dug. When Isaac returned to the land he found the wells closed and dug them again. When he finished digging the wells, he spoke over them naming them the same names as his father had called them. In doing this, he took ownership of them and reclaimed his title, making his property claim sure. He declared the Covenant over his wells because they belonged to him by Covenant right.

There is a story of two brothers who had gone to fight in the US civil war. When they came home, strange people were living on their family land. The squatters had built a little shanty and even planted crops. Neighbors told them that they would have a hard time getting the squatters to leave. The soldiers were given lots of advice on how to remove unwanted tenants, however these two warriors were used to battle and just chased the squatters out.

Just like Isaac and the Civil War soldiers, squatting spirits may come because we are busy doing something else. There is no fault, no conscience sin, just absence. Like the birds that fly over our heads, these squatters come, and because our attention is elsewhere, they take up residence. The fault in this situation is not that they are there, but that they are allowed to stay. We are in a Covenant with God and we have been given ownership of a Covenant land…our promised land. The devil and his demons have no right to squat on our land. They have no right to come into our house trying to take over. They are outside of our Covenant with God and we are obligated to keep our house clean. Don't let them in and

Covenants, by nature, are eternal and perpetual.

if you find them hanging around, chase them away. Don't give them even an inch. Squatting and Trojan spirits will eat all of your fruit. They will till your land and produce their own crops.

> **Joshua 1:13** Remember the word which Moses the servant of the LORD commanded you, saying, 'The LORD your God is providing you a place of rest, and will give you this land. RSV

We are mighty warriors like Joshua. God has given us a promised land of rest. The author of **Hebrews 4:9** tells us that there is a rest for the people of God. That Promised Land belongs to us. It is our home, where we dwell, and where God dwells in Covenant relationship with us. We have been given garments of war and are dressed for battle to protect that land. One of the battles we face is the battle for our own spirit. We must guard our land and keep squatters out.

> **Ephesians 6:13** Therefore take the whole armor of God, that you may be able to withstand in the evil day, and having done all, to stand. NKJV

As I travel from church to church, I have discovered that there are many people who seem to battle the same problems and struggles year after year. Yet there are others, who are immediately set free. Sometimes the people who receive the sudden deliverance seem to have the worst sins and habits, whereas those who struggle have battles that don't seem nearly as severe. I couldn't understand this discrepancy until I understood the difference between Squatters and Trojans. There is a difference

There is a difference between spirits, and some are only removed by tenacious endurance.

between spirits, and some are only removed by tenacious endurance.

My father planted a church in a small Pennsylvania town. Many years before, there had been another church in that borough that had closed its doors. The owners of the church property said that my father could have the building and surrounding land for his new church plant. There was one small problem. Because the church had been closed for many years, the neighbors had taken over the back yard. They had fenced the area and had even planted flowers. Everyone told my dad that these neighbors had "squatter's rights." It was possible that the owners of the church building no longer had any rights at all to that piece of property. One day, while my father was working around the church building, the neighbor who had been tending to the disputed piece of land came over to see him. The man said, "You know, Pastor, I have been using your land. If you want it, take it." The neighbor recognized that the land belonged to the church. Everyone thought the land was his but he knew that it wasn't. By default, the neighbor had been using the land, and now all that my dad had to do was to take it back.

> **Matthew 17:20** He said to them, "Because of your little faith. For truly, I say to you, if you have faith as a grain of mustard seed, you will say to this mountain, 'Move from here to there,' and it will move; and nothing will be impossible to you." RSV

The devil knows that he has no claim on our spiritual house. He knows that all we have to do is to take it back. Our house rightfully belongs to us. Every day, sometimes minute by minute, we have to consciously say yes to the Holy Spirit and declare His authority over us. In **Matthew 17** there was a young man who needed deliverance. Jesus' disciples could not deliver him and asked Jesus to explain to them what they had done wrong. Jesus answered them, "These spirits come out only by prayer and fasting."[8] He could have said squatters are only removed by perseverance and tenacity. Perseverance being a continual appeal to God for deliverance and help. Tenacity being the dogged determination, that no cost or sacrifice is too great in exchange for freedom from these wretched squatters. You have to want a squatting spirit out and you have to be willing to pay the price. This demon is different from other demons and is not easily kicked out! He thinks he has rights. I have no desire to deal with the argument of whether a Christian can be demon possessed or oppressed. Let's just say it's obvious to me that there are Christians who have demonic friends, who have squatted on their "land" and they need to be kicked out!

Chapter 10
Healed Memories

I met Stacy in Bible school. Back then she was a quiet bookworm who seemed very sad. Most of her time was spent working and studying. When I would ask her about her home, she would change the subject, and if pressed, she would only tell bits and pieces. From what I could gather, her stepfather had been hard on her, unforgiving and intolerant. Her parents had divorced and she had been separated from her father, whom she loved. Memories of her birthfather caused her to long for the past. Nightmares had plagued her, causing her to withdraw. I really liked Stacy, but it was hard to get to know her because of the walls she had built around herself.

As students, we were all required to attend a workshop on relationships. As a result of the teachings, Stacy began to feel that the Lord was speaking to her. God asked her to go home and spend some time with her stepfather. She needed to ask him to forgive her for her bad attitude and her part in their broken relationship. At first Stacy was reluctant because she felt she was the only one who had been wronged. But try as she might, she could not get the impression to go home out of her mind. God continued to encourage her to go to her stepfather and ask for his forgiveness, restoring their relationship.

Stacy didn't really want to go home. She told the Lord she couldn't go unless she had a ride and since she lived several hours from the school, she thought that was the end of her problem. Soon after, a student came up to Stacy and told her that he was going home for the weekend. He had found out that Stacy lived close to his home and offered her a ride.

The events were there but the pain was gone. It wasn't repressed memory. It was healed memory.

Going home was difficult for Stacy, because it brought back all the bad memories. Encouraged by the Lord, she asked her stepfather if they could talk. They sat down and Stacy asked the old man if he would forgive her for her part in their broken relationship. Her stepfather said he would forgive her. Then he told her that she was correct in asking for his forgiveness. He berated Stacy's birthfather, making her sorry she had ever started the conversation. He listed all of the things about her natural father that he didn't like, and said she was just like him. Nevertheless, she knew God had sent her. She listened to all he had to say and then told him she was sorry. Little did Stacy know that he would die suddenly, and that she would never have a chance to talk to him again. God's timing had been perfect.

I began to see a difference in Stacy in the days and months that followed. She wasn't so sad anymore. She had a smile on her face. Not only that, but she seemed to blossom into a bright and sociable woman, right before my eyes.

Years later, I had the opportunity to share with a woman's group about the power of God to heal our emotions. I used Stacy as an example. I told them about her experiences growing up and how she had suffered emotionally. I explained to them how she had heard the Lord speak to her. How she had responded to Him by going home and asking for forgiveness from her stepfather. Memories of her sudden transformation flooded my thoughts as I recounted how she had changed right before my eyes.

Stacy's testimony had a powerful impact on the women and I rushed home to call her. I said, "Stacy you won't believe what just happened today. I just shared your testimony with a group of people. I explained to them how terrible your growing up years had been and how God healed you from those memories."

She said, "What are you talking about? I had a wonderful childhood."

In shock I replied, "Stacy! Don't you remember the nightmares you had and the times you used to tell me about. How you hated to go home and that you were afraid?"

There was a short pause and then she said, "I forgot!" She had forgotten. Wonder of wonders… she had forgotten! Later she told me it was like a bad dream. Her mind told her that what I was telling her was true. The events were there but the pain was gone. It wasn't repressed memory. It was healed memory.

Depression is a curse and unforgiveness is like a deep dark pit. Those who live in that pit have no life and become spiritually dead. This becomes a valley of death, where there is no life. It is a place of discontentment and despair. We know that God would not ask us to do something that is impossible. Jesus said in **Mark 11:25-26** that we need to forgive or we won't be forgiven. When we choose to keep anger and hurt bottled up inside, it becomes a cancer to our soul. We become depressed. The joy of life is crushed and there is little for which to live. However when you offer forgiveness, a whole new aspect of eternity is opened to you. You are free. The broken heart is mended and there is hope for tomorrow.

I once heard a famous Bible Teacher say we didn't have to forgive someone if they didn't ask for the forgiveness. I was surprised to hear him say this because forgiveness is fundamental to our walk with Christ. Christ forgave us long before we asked him. Not only does forgiveness free the one who offended us, but also we are set free from the torments of prejudice. Jesus brings forgiveness and freedom.

It is the nature of Jesus to forgive and also to forget. If we are created in the image of God, then we are obligated to *live* as an image of God. This means that every aspect of His nature should be our own, including forgiveness with forgetfulness. Forgetting is an active choice that we make. We must determine in our hearts that we will forget.

People often think that we can't forget, but this is only

because we really don't want to. We think that if we keep the memory alive, we won't fall into another painful experience. Sometimes we choose to remember, because we feel that someone owes us an apology or some kind of retribution. The apology and a desire for justice become so important that our lives become frozen in time, forever stuck in the place of the offense. However, those who walk in forgiveness are mature, rooted in the Love of God, and full of the grace of His Spirit.

The Book of Ruth contains the fantastic story of Ruth, a Moabite woman, who married a Hebrew. We don't know too much about the young man, but we do know quite a bit about his mother, Naomi. Naomi, her husband, and their two sons traveled to the land of Moab because of the famine in their homeland of Judah. The years passed and their lives changed. Naomi's husband died and both sons married Moabite women. Then later, Naomi's sons died making all three women widows. One day, Naomi told her two daughters-in-law that she would return to Judah. Both girls originally said that they would travel with her, but in the end only Ruth made the trip.

Some historians believe that Ruth was the daughter of the King of Moab.[1] This would mean that she had grown up in the palace with all of the privileges that go with it. Marrying one of Naomi's sons would have possibly been a step down in her social standing of the community. I believe that she was drawn by the Holy Spirit to become grafted into a Hebrew family. Obviously, she embraced the God of her new family for in the story she is quoted saying, "Your God shall be my God." There must have been something about Naomi and her familys' relationship to their God that drew Ruth. It had to be extraordinary for her to be willing to leave all of the splendor of her former life behind.

Naomi begged Ruth to stay in the land of Moab. “Go back to your father’s house and marry again,” Naomi had said. Yet Ruth made a Covenant promise with Naomi to stay and travel with her regardless of the cost.

Imagine what it was like for Ruth as she made this journey to a strange new land. Who helped Naomi when the road was rough? Who carried the extra bags? Who hauled the water? Who listened at night for possible danger? Ruth. She was the younger and stronger of the two. She was the one who, as soon as they arrived at Naomi’s former home said, “I will go out and find some food for you to eat.” She was the one who labored in the fields and carried the grain.

When Naomi arrived in her homeland, being greeted by old friends, she said, “Don’t call me Naomi any more. Call me Marra, for I left here full and I have returned empty.” If I had been Ruth standing there I would have felt hurt. Naomi didn’t return empty, she came back with Ruth, her Covenant daughter. Ruth was the one who had traded her glorious past for an unknown future with Naomi. Yet Ruth doesn’t appear to have had any bad feelings toward Naomi. She loved the old woman with her whole heart, working and sacrificing for her. She didn’t whine and complain saying, “Look what I left behind to come with you. Who do you think I am? I have been everything for you and yet you say you came back with nothing?” No! Ruth chose to look forward, and God, who is just, provided for Ruth just as she had provided for Naomi. God not only blessed her by giving her a new husband and a child, but He also gave her a new heritage. Through her son Obed, she became the great grandmother to King David.[2]

In **Ezekiel 47:12** the river of God is described as having fruit trees growing on the banks of that river. Our lives, planted in God's house, will also bear fruit, forgiveness being one of them. These healing trees continually bear fruit and are perpetual. When asked how many times a person should forgive another, Jesus answered with, "seventy times seven," meaning forgiveness is perpetual. Many of us live in the past and won't let it go. We dwell in the land of *could have* and *should have*. Moab, in this story of Ruth, represents the past, our past. Ruth *could have* stayed in Moab, but she would have missed the greatest blessing of her life. She *could have* yearned for her former home and replayed the memories over and over again in her mind. Yet if she had, she would have become bitter and angry. She probably would have starved to death and taken Naomi with her, however she never looked back. She only looked forward, embracing the Covenant she had made with Naomi.

> **Luke 9:62** And Jesus said unto him, No man, having put his hand to the plow, and looking back, is fit for the kingdom of God. KJV

> **Philippines 3:14** I press toward the mark for the prize of the high calling of God in Christ Jesus. KJV

Oswald Chambers, a turn of the century missionary, once said, "Faith for my deliverance is not faith in God. Faith means, whether I am visibly delivered or not, I will stick to my belief that God is love." Chambers' belief in God's love, kept him from being shaken in his faith. He did not allow his natural eyes to divert his assurance in God. He was a man who meditated on the truth and allowed it to develop in him.

Meditation is a powerful word and deserves examination. It means to ponder or to ruminate, to mull thoughts, over and over in your mind. The word ruminate comes from zoology and means to chew partially digested food, swallow, regurgitate, and chew again, like a cow chewing her cud. As disgusting as this may sound, it paints for us a graphic mental picture of meditation. Many phrases come to mind when I think about chewing, "*eat this not that*" or "*you are what you eat"* just to mention a few. When I was a child in elementary school, teachers and parents would say these phrases, as they tried to instill good eating habits. Then, as I grew older and took biology class, I studied food chains and eco systems and discovered the phrase, *"bottom of the food chain"*.

Eating involves chewing, swallowing, and digesting food. What I eat goes through my whole body. Good food makes me healthy and bad food can make me very sick. Years ago, in Africa, I had a wonderful woman who worked for me in my house. She wanted to learn how to cook "American" food, so we spent many hours in my kitchen. She listened to me carefully and tried to cook exactly as I instructed, however we had one ongoing disagreement. She refused to throw away spoiled eggs. If I discovered a spoiled egg and put it in the garbage, she would retrieve it, when I wasn't looking, and use it later. I discovered her secret, but not before she used some bad eggs, in fried rice, causing four people, including her, to have violent food poisoning. She became so sick, she even ended up in the hospital. Needless to say, she didn't use spoiled eggs ever again. Bacteria and parasites may be small and at the bottom of the food chain, but they are very powerful. The bacteria in those few bad eggs had the power to even take a life, if left untreated, and in a strange way, leaving the human body at the "*bottom of their food chain"*.

Meditation is exactly what Paul was talking about, in **2 Corinthians 10:5.** He admonished us to bring every thought into captivity and to the obedience of Christ. He knew that we become what we think about and that if we don't take our thoughts captive, they will enslave us. Have you become the "bottom of the food chain" to your thoughts? Do they devour you every day? Do they eat away at your joy? Do they suck the very life out of you? Who is in control, you or your thoughts?

> **Isaiah 7:9b** If you do not stand firm in your faith, you will not stand at all. NIV

Oswald Chambers understood that he didn't need to be delivered from his problems to have faith, because he wasn't controlled by his thoughts. He was a man who stood firm in his convictions, knowing that regardless of his situation, he was in God's hands. The Bible says that faith comes by hearing, or we could say, eating and meditating. If we eat God's word it becomes a part of us. If we eat sorrow and depression we become sad and depressed. We truly are what we eat.

There is a television commercial about a certain potato chip. It dares the listeners to try and eat just one chip. The idea is that once you start eating, you can't just eat one chip, they will taste so good that you will have to have another. It is the same with thoughts. Once you "eat" or think about a sad thought it is very hard to have only one. The second thought comes to your mind and soon you have eaten the whole bag of sad thoughts. I know some people who live their whole lives only eating sad thoughts. As a result they are sad and lonely people.

The Bible says that faith comes by hearing, or we could say, eating and meditating. If we eat God's word it becomes a part of us. If we eat sorrow and depression we become sad and depressed. We truly are what we eat.

We relate to others using the same thoughts that we have of ourselves. Situations come into our life and because of past experience, we have a predetermined conclusion. I adopted a cat several months ago. When I went to get her, she was a real "scaredy cat". She was hard to catch and even harder to hold. I brought her to our house and she ran and hid under the first piece of furniture she could find. She stayed there until everyone went to sleep. Then she found a new hiding place. It took me several days to locate her. Often the only assurance we had that she was still alive and in the house, was the fact that the food dish was always empty and the litter box was always full. We often had weekend visitors who never even saw the cat and wondered if she was not just a figment of our imagination. I knew the closet where she often hid and I would sit outside the door and pray for her. Soon she ventured out of the closet and became more sociable. Even now, as I write, she is sitting at my feet. Somewhere in this poor feline's past, she had an incident that caused a bad memory. As a result, she had a predetermined conclusion about me and was afraid. I will never know what caused the cat to be afraid, but I do know that good food, love, persistence, and prayer changed her.

> **1 Corinthians 15:19** If for this life only we have hoped in Christ, we are of all men most to be pitied. RSV

> **Jeremiah 29:11** For I know the plans I have for you, says the LORD, plans for welfare and not for evil, to give you a future and a hope. RSV

When something bad happens to us, that event becomes seared on our memory. For some, that memory is so painful that the only way to deal with it, is to run away and pretend it never happened. For others it becomes the center of all other thoughts. Neither is healthy. When we are faced with difficult situations whether past or present, we need to feed our spirit with good thoughts, thoughts of faith, God's word, and hope. We need to meditate on God's love, because "perfect love casts out all fear". We need to remember our Covenant with God and be persistent about taking every thought captive. Bad feelings don't often go away overnight. They seem to stick around, hoping that we will forget our Covenant, give up on our resolution and take the easy road back to despair. Lastly, prayer is critical because it is conversation with the One who knows us best, and hearing God respond to our prayers is what changes who we are.

> **James 4:7** Submit yourselves therefore to God. Resist the devil, and he will flee from you. KJV

When we are faced with difficult situations whether past or present, we need to feed our spirit with good thoughts, thoughts of faith, God's word, and hope.

People in big business know the power of meditation. Paying lots of money, they buy television time devoted solely for the purpose of meditation. Catchy tunes and witty phrases promote their products. Soon we find ourselves singing their praises even if we don't like the thing they are selling. I have found myself singing a song that I didn't particularly like or humming a tune that seemed stuck in my head. The only way to remove those thoughts is by meditating on something else.

We have been told to resist the Devil and he will flee from us, yet often, we have not been told how to do this. The answer is in that which you eat or meditate. The battle for our mind is one many are afraid to fight, but the fight isn't as hard as many people think. It is as easy as changing the things upon which we reflect. We resist the devil when we replace his lies with the Word of God. Remember you become what you ponder. Jesus said, from out of the abundance of the heart the mouth speaks.[3] Your words reveal what you are like inside. If you find yourself thinking and speaking sad depressive thoughts, consider changing your thought diet. Remember your Covenant with Almighty God. Remember who you are and where you live. You live in the house of God and you are the Child of The Almighty. If we remain in Covenant with Him, He has promised that we would always be on the top and never on the bottom.[4] What thoughts are you feeding yourself? The last place I want to be is at "the bottom of the food chain".

Consider the depths of peace we have, when we, in faith, press towards our future. Forgetting the past gives us the courage to look forward. Paul describes, to the church at Philippi, a prize, our eternal home, guaranteed by the Covenant.[5] This reward waits for us at the end of life's journey. Not only that, but Paul also explains to the Corinthians, that if our hope is just for today, we will be miserable; we must place our hope also in the future.[6] If we look back, meditating on the past, we will lose sight of our hope and of our prize. Our future will not look promising if our faith is offended. Don't look back. You can't dwell on your yesterdays if you want a new tomorrow. Don't settle for a life filled with sadness and hopelessness. The Covenant we have with God, promises a future with Him and a today filled with peace, hope, and joy.

Chapter 11
Holiday House

My father and my niece Angelina, visited Fred and I while we were living in Côte d'Ivoire, West Africa. We made a trip, along with some friends, to the far west city of Man, which was quite a distance from our home in Abidjan. Fred was unable to go. While we were on the trip, there was a military coup d'état and the highway entrance to the city of Abidjan was closed. As a matter of fact, all of the highways were closed. As a result my dad, my niece, our friends, and I were obligated to stay in Man for a few extra days.

Not only were the roads shut down but because of the civil unrest, the banks were also closed. I didn't realize until some time later that Fred had been out of money and couldn't get any because of the closed banks. He was lamenting about this when Alphonsine, the woman who lived with us and helped me in my house, told him that I had money hidden under my bed. Fred didn't know where I hid my money. Now, armed with Alphonsine's information, he went looking for my hidden stash. Sure enough, Fred found it right where he had been told to look.

About a year earlier I had started to save some coins. I wanted to buy a few things for my house and thought if I saved my coins that it would give me a good start. Since Fred and I have always traveled a lot in our mission work, I decided that I needed a safe place to hide my money. I had a very nice bed frame made that we set a water bladder inside. I loved my waterbed because, with no heater, it kept my bed nice and cool in the West African heat. I was making the bed one day and realized that, if I lifted the corner of the bladder and shoved my hand as far I could, I could put my saved coins underneath. I figured that no one would ever think to look under hundreds of pounds of water. What a surprise it was to me, when I came home and found that Alphonsine had known about my hidden money. I quickly realized that because Alphonsine lived with us, she had access to the whole house, and knew where everything was.

Fred and I now have a home in New York State, that we jokingly call The Holiday House. We first looked at the house and considered buying it during the Christmas season; we put a purchase offer on the house New Year's Eve day. Then the closing papers were signed the following Easter. We travel so much that often the only time we are there is during a holiday. Nevertheless, that doesn't mean the house is empty. Friends and relatives who need a place to stay often find an empty bed and make our house their home.

I was traveling in Africa once when my dad e-mailed me. He said that he had a guest coming and needed a place for him to stay. "Could my guest stay at your house?" He asked.

I was pretty confident that the living room was neat and clean, and that the guest room was ready for company, but I couldn't remember how the rest of the house looked. I e-mailed my niece, Angelina, and asked her if she would check and see if anything needed to be done before my dad's guest arrived. There had been other visitors since I had gone to Africa and I knew that the house probably needed a little attention. I asked her to spiff up the kitchen and then just "put things away". She told me that she didn't know where I wanted everything put. I told her that it didn't matter. "Just find a spot to hide any odds and ends, and put them away in some closet or bedroom. Then just shut the door." I was hoping my dad's friend wouldn't look behind those closed doors.

Angelina cleaned and rearranged the house until it *looked* clean and tidy for my dad's company. A week later I returned home from the missions trip, happy to see how nice the house looked and also a little surprised with the many odd things hidden behind my bedroom door.

A few months later, another niece, Hannah, moved into our house. It wasn't long before I discovered that I no longer had hiding places. Someone had moved in. I was still in Africa when two women on my ministry team returned to the States early. It's not unusual for our mission teams to congregate at our house before and after trips. Since the women returning early, were Hannah's good friends, the three of them decided to have a sleepover in my bedroom on top of my king sized bed. Everyone was very tired from the flights and my bed was so inviting that the 3 young women spent the whole next day sleeping and lounging in my bed, even having pizza delivered. I later discovered that one of the women needed pajamas to wear and Hannah found some of mine for her to borrow.

There is a big difference between someone who lives in the house, and someone who is just visiting. Whereas before, my visitors only had access to certain parts of my house, now someone had access to even my most intimate places, like my bedroom and my nightclothes. Guests are only allowed to see the best side of things - the rooms we cleaned in advance, and the finest food. They usually have only limited access to closets and personal items. A resident, on the other hand, knows all the secrets. My niece, Hannah, even knows where I hide my chocolate!

I am not offended that people come and go from my house. I don't even mind that some sleep in my bed and use my pajamas. It has shown me a lesson in transparency. I have nothing to hide. May that be true both in my house in New York State, as well as in my spiritual house. I don't want God to only be a visitor. I want him to have the right to come and go from room to room, looking in closets and checking out my secret places.

There is a wonderful transformation that happens to us when we come into a Covenant with God. Not only do we enter into God's house, but God makes his home inside of us. He chooses to live in us. Like someone entering my Holiday House, God arrives at the door of our heart. The question is, "Is He only a guest or is He a permanent resident?"

Jesus said, in **Revelation 3:20**, "Behold, I stand at the door,

There is a wonderful transformation that happens to us when we come into a Covenant with God. Not only do we enter into God's house, but God makes his home inside of us.

and knock: if any man hear my voice, and open the door, I will come in to him, and will eat with him, and he with me." We see two symbols of Covenant in this one illustration. First, the door is opened, with Jesus stepping over the threshold and entering into a blood Covenant. Secondly, Jesus said that after entering, He would eat with the owner of the house, which speaks of forgiveness. When Jesus broke the bread at the last supper, it was a special Covenant ceremony, separate from the Covenant of blood, which is represented by the cup of wine. The Covenant of Broken Bread spoke of forgiveness and of the end of a battle. Fighting no longer, the two Covenant friends can eat together in peace. Eating together speaks of the completion of a Covenant. Only friends lay down past animosities, break bread, and eat together.

Once a Covenant is made with God, He expects to have access to every "room" in our house. Unfortunately there are "rooms" in our lives that we keep "off limits" to God. We "tidy up," pretending that everything is fine, when in reality we have "messes" hidden in secret closets. I have a cupboard in my kitchen that I don't let *just anyone* open. It is full of my plastic storage-wear. Plastic bowls, both round and square with what seems like hundreds of mismatched lids threaten to spill out whenever the door is opened. Like my cupboard full of plastics, our lives often have hidden sins and habits that threaten to spill out should anyone open the door. Fearing rejection, we wonder what will happen if God finds out what we are "really" like inside.

Years ago, my dad was invited to preach at a church which

was several hours from our home. He invited me to travel with him for the weekend. When we arrived at the church, my dad and I quickly noticed the assistant pastor. We actually found it very hard not to stare at him throughout the service. He was the most "plastic" acting person we had ever seen. Pivoting his immaculate head a quarter turn every few seconds, he would randomly gaze at the congregation. On occasion, during the sermon, he would wave a manicured hand as if to indicate his approval.

I wondered who this man was and how anyone could become so artificial. On the outside he looked perfect. With no flaws on the outside, no one could have guessed at the secret turmoil hidden inside. It wasn't until years later that I heard from the senior pastor that his "perfect" assistant actually had many closed doors inside. Shutting the door of his heart to his wife, the senior pastor, and even God, the young man floundered until he lost everything, including his ministry, his wife, and his family. I wondered about this until I realized the significant difference between treating God like a guest or like a resident.

Many people treat God as only a guest. For many years, Fred and I walked around the little town in Pennsylvania where we pastored. Often as we walked, we would stop and talk to other people in our path. One day as we were walking, we could see a woman from our church, standing at the street corner. As we got closer to her, we noticed that she was smoking a cigarette. We knew that she was addicted to cigarettes and she had recently asked us to pray for her. She said she wanted to quit smoking. At first, she didn't see us coming. When she did see

Fearing rejection, we wonder what will happen if God finds out what we are "really" like inside.

us, I could tell by her sudden agitation that she was embarrassed. She didn't want us to see her with a cigarette in her hand. Quickly hiding the offending cigarette, she held it behind her back. Of course, Fred and I had already seen her cigarette. We tried hard not to laugh as little plumes of smoke drifted up from behind her, circling her head.

As Fred and I left the woman, our giggles turned to sadness as we realized how concerned she was about us seeing her with a cigarette. Somehow, she thought that if she could hide the cigarette from us, that she had hidden it from God. When in truth, it didn't matter that Fred and I saw the cigarette, what mattered was that she was trying to shut God out of a "room" in her house.

King Saul tried to shut God out of "rooms" in his house.[1] Saul declared to the prophet Samuel that he had obeyed God when in reality he had disobeyed. He looked like the perfect king. Fighting and defending the children of Israel, he pretended a relationship with the Almighty God. When he decided that he didn't need to follow God's commands and was too important to wait for the prophet Samuel, it became obvious that God was only a visitor in his life. There were times in King Saul's life when he came under the power of the Spirit of God and prophesied. Some people even wondered if Saul was a prophet. Yet in the final days of his life, it became obvious that God had never been welcome in the secret places of Saul's house and sadly, he was known at the end of his life as an enemy of God.[2]

> **Psalms 139:1-3, 23-24** O LORD, You have searched me and known me. You know my sitting down and my rising up; You understand my thought afar off. You comprehend my path and my lying down, And are acquainted with all my ways. Search me, O God, and know my heart; Try me, and know my anxieties; And

> see if there is any wicked way in me, And lead me in the way everlasting. NKJV

“Coming out of the closet” is a phrase that became popular a few years ago. It implies a secret life that is now exposed. I am in a Covenant with God and He lives in my house. I choose to give Him the right to look inside of every closet and behind every closed door. He can check out every corner and rest in any room. I don’t want to be like King Saul and only look good on the outside. In contrast to Saul, King David was comfortable with God knowing every little detail of his life. He invited God to search him, checking even the depths of his thoughts. David asked, “Where can I go from your Spirit? Is there any place I can flee from your presence?”[3] He was not asking God for a place to hide, but he was making a declaration that he had given God complete access to his life. There was no place that God was not welcome.

Chapter 12

Now What?

Often people ask me, "What should I do if I find myself in a bad Covenant?"

My first reaction to that question is one of skepticism. Why does the person think they are in a bad Covenant? Secondly, are they only asking me this question to justify breaking a good Covenant? Many good Covenants go through difficulties that just need to be endured. Yet there are times when something bad is truly happening and something needs to be done. Since every Covenant is different, and goes through times of testing, this can be a hard question to answer.

The Apostle Paul speaks of two Covenants, one of slavery and one of freedom.[1] Of course, Paul is speaking of our former Covenant with death, which is slavery and our current Covenant of life, which is freedom. In this passage, Paul is clear that we should never again submit to the Covenant of Slavery.

> **Galatians 4:24** Now this is an allegory: these women are two covenants. One is from Mount Sinai, bearing children for slavery; she is Hagar. RSV

> **Galatians 5:1** For freedom Christ has set us free; stand fast therefore, and do not submit again to a yoke of slavery. RSV

Having said that, my response is, "Is this Covenant one of Slavery? If you stay, will the Covenant bring about death?"

In my biblical study of Covenant, I find it impossible to justify breaking any Covenants other than the Covenant of Sin and Death. We broke this Covenant, in order to fully embrace the New Covenant of Grace, through the blood of Jesus Christ. I do see where it may be necessary to leave one with whom you have made a Covenant. This is clearly illustrated in the life of David.

David was a man who honored Covenants even when it cost him everything.

David moved into the house of King Saul, soon after he killed the giant Goliath. Things couldn't get any better for the young man. He married the king's daughter, and was best of friends with the king's son, Jonathan. Unfortunately, it was rumored that King Saul wanted to kill David.[2] After hearing from the king's own son, Jonathan, that the rumors were true, David went into hiding. David, the son-in-law to the king, best friends with the king's son, the one who had defended the kingdom, had to run away from his Covenant home. And when he left, he took no one with him. Leaving his wife and best friend, he purposed in his heart to maintain his Covenant. He would never do anything to hurt the king.

This is a hard lesson, because Covenant requires absolute loyalty. If I had been David, I would have been tempted to tell everyone about all of the injustices. I would have at least taken my best friend and spouse with me. Surely no one would expect David to give up everything just because the king had lost his mind and was mad. After all, hadn't the prophet Samuel anointed David to be the next king? Who was King Saul anyway? Saul had lost the presence of God and didn't deserve respect. Even with King Saul clearly in the wrong, David never lifted his hand against the king. Time and time again David found himself in opportunities where he could have broken his Covenant with the king and yet he would not.

Covenants, by nature, are eternal and perpetual. In the story of David and Saul, David chose the road of humility and never ceased to honor the king. Still honoring Saul at the time of his death, David wept and cried, declaring the greatness of King Saul. It is clear that David couldn't continue to live with the king and even had to run and hide from him. However he never broke his Covenant and remained loyal. David would not subject himself to a curse by breaking his Covenant with Saul.

David was a man who honored Covenants even when it cost him everything. Nevertheless, his greatest failure was a broken Covenant with General Uriah. Uriah was a foreigner who swore allegiance to King David and became a general in the Israelite army. There is no Biblical reference of a spoken Covenant between Uriah and David, however it is understood that Uriah would not have risen to the rank of general if he had not vowed to lay down his life for the king. This in itself is indicative of a Covenant.

One year, David chose to remain in his palace while his men went to war.[3] One lonely evening he noticed a beautiful woman by the name of Bathsheba. She was the wife of his friend, Uriah. David requested that Bathsheba come to the palace and he slept with her, stealing his friend's wife. When sometime later she discovered that she was pregnant, she sent word to David. Not knowing what else to do, David sent word for Uriah to return home from the battle. The king was hoping that Uriah would sleep with his wife and then when the baby came, no one would know that the child didn't belong to Bathsheba's husband. The problem was Uriah was a man of honor, who would not enjoy the comforts of home while his fellow soldiers were suffering in the field. No matter how many times David encouraged him to go home, Uriah would not. In desperation, David sent a letter, carried by Uriah himself, to Joab the commander of David's army. The letter instructed Joab to put Uriah at the front of the battle and then pull back, leaving Uriah alone facing the enemy. It was David's desire to have Uriah die in battle. Joab did as David asked and Uriah died. David then took Bathsheba into his home and made her his wife.

Soon, the baby was born and Nathan the prophet came to visit King David. God reminded David of their special relationship, how God had blessed David and had given the entire kingdom of Saul to him. If that had not been enough, God went on to say that He would have given David more. He told David that because he had broken his Covenant by stealing his brother's wife, that the baby would die and that David would suffer the curse of violence and treachery.

David responded by acknowledging his sin before God. He

cried out to the Lord and his prayer is known today as Psalms 51. In this song he begged God not to leave him, and asked God to give him a clean heart, making his spirit right. He must have remembered the hours he spent playing music to sooth the anguished mind of the mad King Saul. Fearing that the Holy Spirit might leave him like He left Saul, David cried out to God, admitting his sin. David knew, more than anyone else, the absolute horror and turmoil King Saul experienced because of his disregard for his Covenant with God. David spent most of his life pursuing God and understood Covenant. He knew that if he would come to God with a broken and contrite heart, that God would not reject him. His Covenant with God was unbreakable and unchangeable. The only thing that would break his Covenant with God would be an unrepentant and hard heart. David knew better than to offer the blood of bulls and goats. He knew there would be no sacrifice acceptable, other than his own living sacrifice.

He knew that if he would come to God with a broken and contrite heart, that God would not reject him. His Covenant with God was unbreakable and unchangeable.

There is a remarkable end to David's story. David's Covenant was restored with God, and as a result, God made some incredible promises to David. Through the prophet Nathan, God told David that he would have a son who would sit upon his throne. Not only that, but God promised that He would establish David's throne forever. David, in astonishment, responded to God's promise by asking God if that is how He deals with man. Would God really make an eternal Covenant with David, His greatest failure?[4] This Covenant, called a Covenant of Salt, was an eternal perpetual Covenant. David found it hard to believe that God would give him such an unbelievable gift. As extraordinary as this was, the promise did not stop there. The son who would sit upon the throne of David would be none other than the son of Bathsheba. God was able to take David's broken Covenant with Uriah and turn the whole situation into an eternal Covenant that would be a blessing and a sign of forgiveness to both David and generations throughout eternity.

Whereas David had to leave his Covenant friend, Shadrach, Meshach and Abednego had to stay in their difficult situation. When our son Christopher was small, the account of these three young Hebrew men was his favorite bedtime story. He loved to hear about the bravery of the godly young men. Night after night he would say, "Daddy, read about Shadrach, Meshach and Abednego."[5] Children of Judah, they were carried captive into Babylon. Nebuchadnezzar forced them into servitude but quickly elevated them to a prominent place of employment.

Nebuchadnezzar was an arrogant evil king who not only worshipped many gods but declared himself to be equal with God. Setting up a golden image of himself, he forced all of his subjects to worship him. On a regular schedule, royal musicians played a tune, which signified to everyone that they should bow down and worship the king's image. Anyone who dared refuse this command would be thrown into a fiery furnace.

Our three young heroes refused to bow down and worship the king's golden image. They would only worship the Lord God Almighty. There were people in the land who were jealous of Shadrach, Meshach and Abednego. They complained to the king and told Nebuchadnezzar that the Hebrew men refused to bow down and worship his golden image. They also reminded the king of the punishment reserved for those who refuse to bow down. All who disobey must be thrown into the fiery furnace.

When the king heard this information, he was angry and called for Shadrach, Meshach and Abednego. “Is it true?” he asked them, “Have you really disobeyed me?” After all, Shadrach, Meshach and Abednego had been given good positions in the kingdom and were well known by the king. Nebuchadnezzar couldn’t believe that anyone would disobey his edict, especially these three young men. He told them he would give them another chance and that when the music was played they must bow down and worship him, and his golden image, or suffer the consequences.

Without a moment’s hesitation the three answered the king, “O Nebuchadnezzar, we are not afraid. If you choose to throw us into your blazing furnace, our God, whom we serve is able to deliver us. He can protect us, even from you, but even if He doesn’t, we still refuse to bow down and worship your gods and your golden image.”

Knowing that their Covenant with God was higher than any relationship or Covenant they may have had with King Nebuchadnezzar, Shadrach, Meshach and Abednego, chose to rely on their Covenant Redeemer. Without fear, they stood before the king and declared that God would fulfill His obligations to them. Even if they died, they would never break their Covenant with God by worshiping another.

The king was so angry at their response that his face was contorted with rage. He ordered the furnace to be heated seven times hotter than it had been and commanded guards to bind Shadrach, Meshach and Abednego and throw them quickly into the furnace. The fire was so hot that the guards who threw the young men into the fire died from the flames and from the heat.

The king stood gazing into the fire, anxious to see the Hebrew men burn, when he saw an amazing sight. Turning to his aids he asked them, “Didn’t we throw three men into the fire?” “Yes,” came the reply.

Peering deeply into the fire the king said, “Look there are four men walking in the fire. The fourth man looks like the Son of God!”

As Shadrach, Meshach and Abednego were thrown into the fire, the ropes that bound them burned off and they were free. As if there were no fire at all, the three walked about, accompanied by the Son of God. God, their Covenant Redeemer, honored their faith and walked with them, fulfilling the Covenant.

Nebuchadnezzar called out, “Shadrach, Meshach and Abednego, servants of the Most High God, come out!”

So the three young Hebrews walked out of the fire. Everyone came to look at them. In astonishment they discovered that Shadrach, Meshach and Abednego had no burns and didn’t even smell like smoke. The fire had not touched them, their way out was into the fire but the fire only burned off the ropes that had them bound. The king then declared that there was no God like the God of Shadrach, Meshach and Abednego.

We can trust that our Covenant Redeemer will walk with us and keep us, even in the middle of our greatest nightmares.

Sometimes there is no way out of a situation. Obligated to stay, a person has to trust in their Covenant with

To redeem something means to exchange it for something else. Jesus, our Covenant Redeemer, exchanged His life for ours.

God. Countless times, God has walked with me through the fire. Troubles and trials come and just like the story of Shadrach, Meshach and Abednego, we are thrown into the midst of the inferno. Our Covenant with God is greater and more powerful than any fire. We can trust that our Covenant Redeemer will walk with us and keep us, even in the middle of our greatest nightmares. We are not always delivered out of the fire, but we have a promise that our God will never leave us or forsake us and like the three young men, we can walk out of the fire without even the smell of smoke.[6]

David found himself in a situation where he had to leave his Covenant friend, King Saul. Shadrach, Meshach and Abednego on the other hand, had to stay and face the fire. In both circumstances, God redeemed the situation. Even David's broken Covenant with Uriah could be redeemed.

To redeem something means to exchange it for something else. Jesus, our Covenant Redeemer, exchanged His life for ours. Our old life, with its bad and broken Covenants, has been replaced. Have hope in God no matter your situation. God can and will walk with you through your difficult time. He will restore you and give you a new and everlasting Covenant. When faced with his greatest failure, David called out to his God and said, "Create in me a clean heart, oh God, and renew a right spirit in me." God heard the cry of David's heart and created not only a new heart and a new spirit but also a New Covenant. God gave David an eternal Covenant that would span all of Eternity. Through the brokenness of David's life came a Covenant that would bring salvation to you and to me. God redeemed even Bathsheba and through her lineage was born, Jesus, the son of David, our Covenant Redeemer.[7]

David, in awe of God's goodness to him, asked, "Oh God, is this how you deal with man? Are you really so good, that you would exchange all of my failures for an eternal Covenant?"

God's answer was, "Yes!"

Through the brokenness of David's life came a Covenant that would bring salvation to you and to me.

Chapter 13

He Came Looking For Me

The middle of the swamp was dark and creepy. Owls hooted in the distance while a frog sang his lonely song in the puddle at her feet. At seven years old, Cheri wasn't very big, but she was brave. "Stay right there," her father had said. "I forgot my gun. Here's a lantern. Sit on this stump while I go back to the truck, but remember, don’t be afraid. I'll be right back."

He was gone only a few minutes when Cheri, swinging her foot, caught the handle of the lantern and tipped it over.

They had come to the swamp in the darkest part of the night, which was when the raccoon would be out. Now with the lantern gone out, it was really dark. Cheri loved "coon" hunting with her dad. She had been hunting many times and she trusted her daddy, even if it was dark, cold, and creepy.

Sometime later her father ,returning but not seeing the light from the lantern, began to call out, "Cheri, where are you?"

"Over here," she replied.

"What happened to the lantern?"

"Oh, it fell over and the light went out," came her answer.

"Weren't you afraid?" her father asked.

"No, I knew you would come," came her matter-of-fact reply.

If I have heard this story once, I have heard it a hundred times. Cheri is my sister, and it was my dad who left her in the middle of the swamp. What keeps a seven-year old from being terrified while alone in the middle of a dark and creepy swamp? Why wasn't she crying and hysterical when her dad returned? This kind of peace cannot be forced upon a person with words like, "Don't be afraid." It is a learned peace that comes from experience.

Years ago, my son was making some hard decisions about his future. Knowing that he was frustrated with the whole decision making process, I called him to see if he had come to any conclusions. His response was, “Mom, I’m walking in the dark and holding onto the hands of Jesus real tight.”

Even today, I am struck by the wise simplicity of his words. Like my sister Cheri, he had a learned peace that came from experience.

> **Matthew 13:45-46**, Again, the kingdom of heaven is like a merchant seeking beautiful pearls, who, when he had found one pearl of great price, went and sold all that he had and bought it. NKJV

The Kingdom of God is like a merchant, seeking for pearls of great value. Jesus is the merchant; you are the pearl. Like a man who goes out searching for great treasure, Jesus began searching for you. His eyes spanned all of time, past and present. Then he saw you. He saw who you were, what you had become, and what you could be. He saw a treasure that was worth giving all that he had. He saw a treasure worth giving his life for…YOU!

One day while driving to work, my sister heard the Lord say that she was special. He told her that he loved her more than anyone else. She was surprised, and asked the Lord, "How can this be? How can you love me more than anyone else? I don't understand."

The Lord then explained to her about His nature. He is omnipresent…meaning He is everywhere at all times, and omniscient…meaning He knows all. Then He said, "I am also *omniexclusive*. I can love each person exclusively more than anyone else."

Perhaps you have never thought about God in this way, however, you **are** loved. You are not only loved, but you are loved more than anyone else. You are that pearl of great price. Jesus sold all he had to purchase you. He left heaven, was born like you and I, and took the body of a man. He suffered, shed his own blood, and died that you could become His. He came looking for you. He is the greatest treasure seeker and you are His treasure.

I have noticed that some people don't realize the depth of God's love for them. Their concept of "Father love" is warped. Past experiences tell them that their Father God is the same as a natural father. If their father beat, abused, ignored, or deserted them, then their heart tells them Father God is the same. Because of this belief, they are unable to see the truth. These wounded people need a new understanding of who God is. He is their loving and caring Father, who sees them as a great treasure. He sacrificed His beloved son, Jesus, His most cherished possession.

I have wonderful memories of my dad that have helped me understand my Heavenly Father. These memories help define my understanding of Father God and give me a confidence in trusting Him. Unfortunately, many have never had experiences like I did. When I was sixteen years old, I received my driver's license. I was very eager to drive and often volunteered to go on errands. One day my mom needed some milk for dinner and asked me to go get some. I went to get the milk, but being a new driver, I didn't look at the gas gauge. On the way home I ran out of gas. I coasted to the side of the road, rolled up my windows, and locked all of my doors. I sat in the car and waited, because I knew that if I waited, my dad would come looking for me.

When I didn't come home, my dad began to wonder where I was. He and my grandfather left the house to look for me. All this time I was just waiting in the car, knowing that my dad would come. As they drove past where I was parked, my grandfather said to my dad, "Isn't that your car?"

Sure enough it was his car and I was inside. My dad came

to the window and said, “Deb, what are you doing here?”

I answered, “I’m just waiting for you. I knew you would come.”

I didn’t realize the impact that incident made on my life until many years later, on my first trip to the Far East of Russia. Fred and I had traveled many days, just to reach the Far East of Russia, and the Bible school where we were going to be the directors. Upon arriving, the pastor took us to the campground where the Bible school and our bedroom were located. We dropped off our luggage and then traveled into the city where the pastor lived. He fed us a nice meal and then proceeded to explain the projects of the school.

After a while, the conversation changed from Bible school details to computer needs and I quickly excluded myself from the discussion. It became apparent to me that this could go on for a while and I was tired. I asked the pastor if he would take me back to the school where I could rest. Leaving me there, He assured me he would bring Fred back to the school when they were finished talking over his computer problems.

When I first saw my room, there had not been a working lock on my door (I didn’t know that in my absence it had been fixed). So after Fred and the pastor left me at the door of my room, I didn’t even try to lock it. I laid down and went fast asleep.

Waking up in the early evening, I wondered where Fred was. Realizing he was still working on computers, I went back to sleep. Then, around midnight I awoke again. Still again Fred wasn’t there. This time I needed to use the toilet

Nothing kept my Heavenly Father from being with me when I spent my first night, seemingly alone in Russia. I was in Covenant with Him and He would always be there for me.

and had to find my way outside in the dark, to the one and only out-house. Returning to my room, I wondered where Fred was but still didn't panic, and I went back to sleep.

Now, for you to fully appreciate this story you have to understand, there was no phone at the school and I had never been in that part of the country before. I didn't know a single person at the school and I spoke no Russian. I continued to sleep and wake at intervals until morning came and still, there was no Fred. Suddenly I realized that school was about to start and the students were gathering in the classroom. I joined them, and by crude hand motions asked a young man to start the students singing. There was no translator, no pastor, and still, no Fred!

After about twenty minutes of singing, the pastor and Fred arrived. Poor Fred. He had wanted to come to me, but un-beknownst to the both of us, the pastor had no intention of bringing Fred to the school later. Because it was late at night, the streets were closed and he had locked his car in a garage. Fred knew I was waiting for him, but he had no way to communicate with me. I had spent my very first night in the Far East of Russia, alone!

Looking back on the situation, I was pleasantly surprised that I had not panicked. I wasn't scared. I had just slept and waited. It wasn't until later that I realized the expecta-tions I had of my earthly dad influenced my belief in my Heavenly Father. The day I sat in the car and waited for my father to come find me, and he did come, prepared me for that night in Russia. As I waited in my room, all alone, I had nothing to fear. I felt the presence of God with me and I waited. Just as nothing would have prevented my earthly dad from coming to look for me when I had gone to buy milk, nothing kept my Heavenly Father from being with me when I spent my first night, seemingly alone in Russia. I was in Covenant with Him and He would always be there for me.

What you believe determines your response to your situations. When something happens to you, whether it is a good or bad, you have certain beliefs. Those beliefs determine your reactions. I was alone in Russia. I believed that my loving Heavenly Father never leaves me, and always takes care of me. Therefore, I was not afraid. I would have been afraid, had I believed that I was worthless and that no one cared. If I believed that my natural father cared nothing about me and wouldn't come looking for me if I were in trouble, then those thoughts would have flooded my mind that night. Because I firmly believed that my Father loved me, I was not afraid!

We need to change our unhealthy belief systems. We need to tell ourselves the truth and find the freedom it brings. The Bible says that it is the truth that will set us free. The truth is, you are a treasure and Jesus died for you. He gave His life just for you. You are the treasure he was seeking after, and He gave up everything just to purchase you.

He invested not only his earthly life in you, but His Spirit so you could become all he knows you can be. He has great plans for your special life. The dreams He placed in you are not just to imagine and hope for, but they are to propel you into a lifelong adventure. He won't dangle hopes before you and then laugh when they seem out of reach. He loves you and wants to help fulfill all of your hopes and dreams.

It is during the difficult times of our life, that we find the tools we need to fulfill the desires of our hearts. If we believe that God hates us and is punishing us, then while we are in a difficult situation, we won't even try and believe for good things. We will cry and ask God, "Why? Why me? What Have I done? Oh God, why do you hate me?" However, if you have told yourself the truth, and know that *All things work together for our good*, then you will know that in the darkness, God has hidden treasures.[1] It is in the darkness that our light is revealed. If you know that you are loved and that you are the treasure God seeks, that you were hidden in the darkness of Sin and that God dug deep to find you, if you know that you are loved and have been created in the image of God, you too will dig deep into the darkness and look for treasure. You will stop looking at your troubles as "bad things happening to me" and begin to see them as an opportunity to find treasure. When you come into Covenant with God, you know that no matter what your situation is, you live in His house.

Moses explains, in the book of Deuteronomy, the blessings that come into our lives because of the Covenant we have with God. He also describes the curses that fall upon us should we choose to reject God's loving welcome, and break our Covenant with Him. Moses said, "Today I set before you a blessing and a curse. What you receive is your choice."[2] In every situation we have the opportunity to choose a blessing or a curse. A few years ago, my friend Cathy's house burned down. It was a total and devastating loss. The other day she said to me, "You know, my husband and I have received so many blessings from the loss of our house." She went on to recount all of the good things that had come out of their fire. She chose to look for a blessing instead of a curse. Listening to her, I thought how bitter and sad she could have become had she spent these last few years mourning her loss. Instead, she was listing the treasures she had found in her dark place.

We all have opportunities to choose. I was complaining about some people and situations one day, when my husband Fred said to me, "Don't go there, don't be that kind of person." Feeling a little condemned and attacked, I started to tell him that he had no business telling me how to think. Then all of a sudden, I realized the wisdom in his statement. When something goes wrong, when bad things happen, remember who you are and where you live. Don't take yourself out of God's house by grumbling and complaining. Don't go into the land of unforgiveness, doubt, and confusion. It is a place that you don't want to go. Don't allow your thoughts to make you into someone you don't want to be. When you are tempted to believe unhealthy thoughts, just take some advice from Fred. Say to yourself, "Don't go there. Don't be that person." It's a blessing or a curse, you can choose.

When you come into Covenant with God, you know that no matter what your situation is, you live in His house.

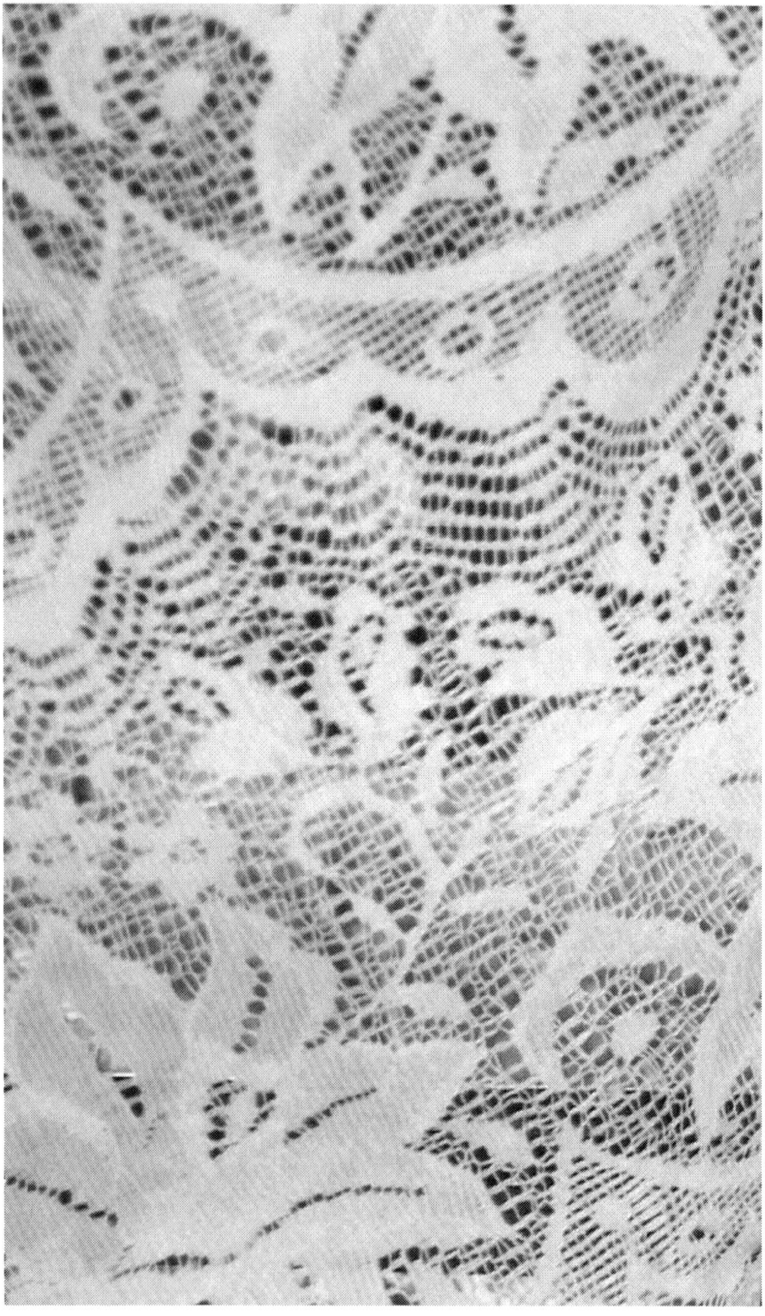

Chapter 14

It's In There

Psalms 103:1-2 Bless the LORD, O my soul: and all that is within me, bless his holy name. Bless the LORD, O my soul, and forget not all his benefits. KJV

1 Peter 1:6 In this you rejoice, though now for a little while you may have to suffer various trials. RSV

The Lord spoke to the Apostle Paul during a night vision where he saw a Macedonian man begging for Paul to come and help him.[1] Paul and his friend, Silas wanted to go to Bithynia, however out of obedience to God, and being directed in the vision, they went to Macedonia instead. When they arrived in Macedonia, some local people were unhappy with their ministry and the magistrates of the city had Paul and Silas thrown into prison. It was not their choice to go to Macedonia however, they went out of obedience to do God's work, and now they were in prison. Prisons at that time were not nice places. They were dark and dirty holes in the ground with rats and bugs and probably even snakes. Having been beaten, their backs were sore and bleeding. Paul had a desire to preach the Gospel, start churches, and win many to Christ in Macedonia. However, it seemed as if his desires would never become a reality.

Human nature would demand an answer from God for this situation. In frustration and discouragement many would cry out to God and ask "why?" Wondering if they had missed God's plan or made a mistake about going to Macedonia, some might even accuse God, asking why He would be so cruel as to put "me" in prison, when "I" obeyed Him, instead of doing what "I" wanted to do.

> **Psalms 145:18-19** The LORD is near to all who call upon him, to all who call upon him in truth. He fulfils the desire of all who fear him, he also hears their cry, and saves them. RSV

This is not what Paul and Silas did. They knew that everything they needed was in God's house. At midnight, when it is the darkest time of the night, our two Apostles began singing and praising God. They prayed, trusting in the God who had ordered their steps. Suddenly, in the midst of their worship, there was a great earthquake. The earth shook, the prison shook, the prisoners shook, and so did their chains, till all the prisoners were free. Reading this story, in the book of Acts chapter 16, shows us that everyone was freed from their chains. The jailor, who was responsible for the prison, was afraid that he had lost all of his prisoners. This was a failure worthy of death, and in fear of the magistrates, he pulled out his sword to kill himself. Paul saw the jailor and called out, "Stop! Don't be afraid, we are all here." In the middle of the prison, in the middle of Paul and Silas' dark night, they received the desire of their heart. The jailor and his whole family were saved. The two apostles spoke the Word of the Lord and everyone in the house became a follower of Jesus. They had a revival. Inside of Paul's prison was exactly what he wanted.

Paul was a student of the scriptures and knew the words of King David. David often told his soul what to do, as we see in **Psalms 103:2**. Deep in the night, like David, Paul told his soul what to do. He worshiped the Lord, praising Him in spite of his surroundings. Inside of Paul's prison was what Paul truly wanted and while he was telling himself what to do, God was busy giving it to him. Paul understood, that in difficult situations, he had to tell his soul what to do. And when he did…well…he got just what he wanted.

The same is true for you and I. Everything we need is in God's house. You have stepped over the blood of Christ and have entered into an eternal home. The Covenant you made with God provides more than just a list of do's and don'ts. It includes a love that says, "I want to see my Covenant friend happy." We have come into Covenant with a God who wants to see us happy and who wishes to give us the desires of our hearts.

> **Psalms 37:4** Take delight in the LORD, and he will give you the desires of your heart. RSV

When my son Christopher was small, he loved the plastic building blocks called LEGOS. He collected as many as he could get. One year, when he was about 8 years old, he asked for one particular expensive set for Christmas. It was the only thing he wanted. We didn't have enough money for that set and tried in vain to tempt him with cheaper toys. Everyday he would declare that that particular LEGO set was all he wanted. He even went so far as to say he would

We have come into Covenant with a God who wants to see us happy and who wishes to give us the desires of our hearts.

be happy if it were the only item he received for Christmas, from everyone in the family including, grandmas, grandpas, aunts and uncles. So I started asking my family members if they would like to give money towards Christopher's gift. Everyone in the family helped, and Fred and I went to the store to buy the coveted LEGO set.

I like to have all of my Christmas presents bought and wrapped early. I don't like to wait for the last minute, so I often wrap each present as I buy it. Then I bring them out as soon as I get my tree up and leave the pretty packages under the tree. Fred and I had the LEGO set hidden in the house. This present caused a small problem for me. I didn't want Christopher to know what was in his package and LEGOS are pretty easy to figure out. The box, all wrapped up, was just the way Christopher pictured it in his mind. Also the noise it made, when shook, gave the unmistakable sound of plastic LEGOS pieces moving around inside. I really didn't want to set the wrapped box under the tree, because I wanted this present to be a surprise. If I didn't put anything under the tree with Christopher's name on it, he would wonder why there was nothing for him.

Finally I had an idea. I sent Fred to a department store to look for a big box, something about the size of a large TV set. He came home with the perfect carton and I set to work disguising Christopher's gift. I reopened the LEGO box and filled it with extra Styrofoam packing, so when shook, the box would not make any noise. Then I resealed the original box. Then I laid several bricks in the bottom of the larger box, set the LEGO box in, and finished filling the larger box with old bath towels. Wrapping the big box with the prettiest paper and finishing the top with a large bow, I dragged (because it was now too heavy to carry) the box out into the living room and placed it under the tree.

As soon as Christopher saw the box, with his name on it, he began to cry. He cried and cried. Nothing I could do would make him happy. Sobbing, he said, "It's not what I wanted. It's not what I wanted. I know what a LEGO box looks like and this is not it! It is not what I wanted!"

No matter what I said, Christopher would not be happy. He was sure his Christmas was spoiled. I really didn't want to tell him that there was a wonderful LEGO set in the box because it would spoil the surprise. I kept saying, "Don't worry, you will get something wonderful. You're going to get just what you want." I pleaded, "Trust me. You will be very happy when you open this present. It's a very nice present. You will like it when you see it."

No matter what I said, he would just look pitifully at the box and say, "No! This isn't what I want."

We had to wait two weeks until Christmas and I didn't know what to do. I had wrapped Christopher's present so it would be a surprise, but now the surprise was making Him miserable. I regretted the whole situation and now, it was too late. All we could do was wait for Christmas to arrive. Of course you can well imagine Christopher's joy when he opened the box and realized his dream had really come true. This huge confusing box was really just what he wanted.

Often I see people who are disappointed with their life. They are dissatisfied with their "box", and don't realize that what they want is carefully enclosed within their situation. If they would only trust God, they would see that it *is* just what they wanted. How often have you been angry with God, railing accusations, crying tears of frustration, saying things like, "This isn't fair! I didn't sign up for this. I trusted God for better things."

I have also had "boxes" that I didn't like. A few years ago when we were living in the Ivory Coast, I felt we needed a bigger house. Fred and I were on a small budget and didn't think we could afford a bigger house. I began looking for one in the same price range as we were already paying. Fred said we could get a bigger house if it was the same amount of money. I found exactly what I wanted and inquired of the price. I was not really surprised when the woman responded with more than 3 times the amount of money we had. After a long series of negotiations and lots of prayer, the woman finally agreed to give us the house for our ridiculously low offer. Unfortunately, there was about to be a civil war in that country. After a few short months, we had to leave and my heart was broken. I really loved my house. I had prayed for that house. I had decorated it and made it my home. It was just what I had wanted. I didn't want to leave the country but mostly I didn't want to lose my home.

The last five days in my home were the hardest. I sorted and packed all of the things I had collected through the years that make a house homey. There was a girl's home where I wanted to send most of my things so I started to bag and box my clothes. As I packed, I couldn't stop myself from crying. Then I remembered **Psalms 103:2**. I said to myself, "I have to tell myself what to do!" So I went to my bedroom, sat on my bed and started telling myself to be obedient to the Word of the Lord. I literally beat my chest and said, "Soul, you bless the Lord." Then I stood up, started singing, and forcing myself through my tears, to praise the Lord. I started to feel better and went back to packing. Unfortunately, when I started to box my books to give them away, I started to cry again. So off to my bedroom I went and told my soul what to do, until I could return to packing. Everyday it was the same. Pack, cry, tell my soul to bless the Lord, sing, feel better, go back to packing, and the cycle would start all over again.

On the day before we left, during one of my crying-singing-blessing moments, God began to speak to me. He whispered in my heart and said; "I have never asked you to give up something that I have not replaced with something better. I'm going to give you another home. You will no longer rent, but this time you will own your house, and it will be just what you want." I excitedly told Fred what had just happened and what God said.

As we were traveling the next day, across West Africa, we stopped at a crusade where a friend was speaking. When we arrived and our friend saw us, he turned to Fred and whispered something in his ear. Fred's eyes got big and he said to him, "You have got to tell this to my wife." Our friend turned to me and told me how he and his wife were selling property. They had been praying about what to do with the money, God had told them to give me some of the money to buy a house. While I was blessing the Lord, God had been speaking to this couple. While I was choosing to trust God and telling my soul what to do, God was buying a house for me.

I said to myself, "I have to tell myself what to do!" So I went to my bedroom, sat on my bed and started telling myself to be obedient to the Word of the Lord.

Remember, your situation is only temporary. We all have times when it would be easier to cry. As a matter

Our Covenant says that we will be blessed. A key to unlocking that blessing is "Telling Yourself What to Do".

of fact, I did not want to bless the Lord while I was packing up my house. I wanted to cry and make everyone in the house hear and feel sorry for me. But I chose to bless the Lord and trust in Him. God had something for me in the middle of my dark time. In the middle of Paul's prison was what he wanted. In the middle of my packing was what I wanted. On Christmas day, inside of Christopher's box, was what he wanted.

Choose to bless the Lord. If you look at your situation and say, "I made a Covenant with God and this box, (my current situation), isn't what I expected." Then, have hope in your Covenant. In your finances, bless the Lord. In your marriage, bless the Lord. In your family, bless the Lord. At your job, bless the Lord. The Covenant guarantees that our Covenant Redeemer will fight for us. Our Covenant says that we will be blessed. A key to unlocking that blessing is "Telling Yourself What to Do". The day will come when you will open your box and see that what is inside, is just what you wanted. Rejoice. It's in there.

Chapter 15

Hopes, Dreams, and Reality

Fred and I returned from an exciting mission trip to Russia and Belarus just eleven days before Christmas. We had been contemplating a change in our occupation, from being pastors to overseas missionaries. The trip to St Petersburg, Moscow, and Minsk had been very exciting. Over and over in my mind, as I prepared for Christmas day, I relived the visits to the Kremlin, Saint Basil's Cathedral, The Hermitage, and The Palace of Peter the Great. Amid the hustle and bustle of baking and house cleaning, I pushed aside feelings of weariness, interpreting it as "jet lag". Anyone would be tired, traveling like we had, and jumping right into the holidays.

The morning after Christmas, Fred, Christopher, and I prepared to celebrate the holidays at Fred's mother's house and loaded the car for the three-hour drive. As I settled into the car, I noticed that something was very wrong. I told Fred that I didn't feel well and that we had to change our plans. Instead of driving to my mother-in-law's house we went to the emergency room. That day I hemorrhaged and lost one third of my blood. After many hours, the emergency room doctors decided that I had a hormonal imbalance. I was only thirty-eight years old and there seemed no other explanation for such profuse bleeding. They sent me home with medication, told me to rest, and to drink plenty of fluids.

Two weeks later, I was still bleeding. This time I went to see a specialist. She did more tests. Fred and I planned to travel to Florida for a conference the next week. The doctor told us to go ahead with our plans. "Just take it easy," she said. "I'll call you if I find any problems with your test results."

A few weeks later, in the early hours of the morning, Fred and I returned home from our trip. As we entered our house, we were greeted by numerous beeps, indicating messages on our telephone answering machine. They were from my doctor saying, "Call me as soon as you get this message." We called the doctor and she instructed us to meet her, that minute, at the hospital where she was working. She told us the shocking news. I had cancer. Because of my age, the type of cancer had the doctor baffled, and she arranged for me to see a Gynecologic Oncologist the next day. The specialist confirmed the first doctor's suspicions; it was cancer. I was scheduled for surgery four days later.

In shock and fear, Fred and I returned to our home. I felt

totally unprepared to hear the dreaded "C" word. Would I die and if I did, what would happen to my sixteen-year old son? How would he handle this situation? What about my husband? How would he deal with this? I feared for everyone; I feared for myself. A black cloud of apprehension covered my heart like a blanket, wrapping me in despair. What about all of my hopes and dreams? Was this the end of my life? For two days I sat in a chair, with a blanket wrapped around me. I just couldn't believe this was happening to me. The battle in my spirit was of monumental proportions. My mind couldn't wrap itself around the facts I had just heard. The devil screamed accusations against God in my ears and I felt like I was drowning in a sea of despair. God just kept whispering in my heart, "Trust Me."

I made a decision that day. I had trusted God all of my life and I wasn't about to stop. I now had only two more days until my scheduled surgery. The next day was Sunday and I intended to declare my faith and trust in the Lord Jesus, who had given his life for me. If Shadrach, Meshach and Abednego could face the fiery furnace of King Nebuchadnezzar and not lose their faith, then I would face my fiery trial in faith too. I stood before our congregation that Sunday morning and sang with all of my heart and conviction, "What a faithful God, Have I." I made a public declaration that whether I lived or died, I would never stop loving and trusting my Lord Jesus. I had a radical hysterectomy on February third and six days later, returned home to recover.

While I was recuperating at home, my friends and family came to help Fred and Chris take care of me. They cleaned the house and cooked food. I was barely able to walk and some days, I even needed help eating. It was one of those days that my friend, Thelma, called me on the telephone. While Fred and I had been in Florida, I made plans to travel in March with Thelma and her husband, Lou. They were gathering a prayer team to go to North Africa. As soon as I heard about their trip, I felt in my heart that I was supposed to go. I told Thelma that I would, but now I was recovering from surgery and I also needed to have further radiation treatment. "Lou and I have been praying about our trip," she said excitedly. "We really feel that you are a part of our team and if you think you will be well enough to travel, we will postpone the trip one month."

I asked Thelma when she needed my answer. Her reply was, "I have a travel agent holding a ticket for you right now. Her office closes in fifteen minutes."

I told her to buy the ticket. I would go. I still had to have radiation treatments, and I had to regain my strength. My surgeon would not be happy since he had told me it would take me three months before I could resume my life, but I didn't care. The trip was about six weeks away. God was birthing a new hope in me and excitement began to flood my heart.

I had the radiation, which was a nightmare all of its own. Yet it didn't stop my determination to go on that trip. God had told me to go and I was going. Fred and Christopher walked with me everyday. Up and down our street they walked, one on each side of me, supporting me in my renewed hopes and dreams.

The trip was supposed to be a simple prayer journey. The plan was that we would stay in the home of missionaries and make day trips into the city. However when we arrived, the missionary had exciting news. He had been granted vacation time at his secular employment. Now instead of easy day trips to the city, we would go backpacking all over the country, seeing and praying for as many cities and villages as we could in eight days. I was able to walk, but back packing? Don't worry Lou and Thelma said, "We'll carry your back pack." And they did. Everyone on the team helped me, from carrying my things to even carrying me. Once while racing for a bus, Lou and the missionary, John, carried me up, what seemed like, a mountain of stone steps. Up we flew, reaching the bus station just in time. It was a life-changing trip and I returned home with a renewed passion to go into mission work fulltime.

God just kept whispering in my heart, "Trust Me."

A little less than a month after I returned home, Fred made his third trip to Russia and also to the Ukraine. Home schooling our son, pastoring the church, and recovering from my trip, I "held down the fort" until Fred came home. It was now the month of May.

When Fred returned, he and I spent quite a bit of time praying about our future. Life held a new meaning for me and I didn't want to waste it. Fred had fallen in love with the Bible School in Russia. We had been offered a position at the school. We would direct the school and also teach at it. Our son was finishing High School that year and he decided to go to Bible School in New York. With a confidence that God was in our plans, we gave our church three months notice. We told them that we would be leaving and moving to Russia.

Through the years, I had been given so many things that I couldn't bring myself to sell anything, so I informed all of my family and friends that we were selling our house and that I was giving almost everything away. I packed some boxes and filled the corner of my mom and dad's attic with mementos and then told people to come and get what they wanted. We listed our house with a realtor and the first person that looked at it agreed to our asking price. Soon the house was sold and everything was gone.

The end of August came and it was time for Christopher to get settled in at school. We took our only son to Bible School and started the horrible season of the "empty nest." It was an odd time in our life. We were changing occupations, giving up our home and possessions, sending our only child off to school, and moving to a strange country. At the same time I was still recovering from my surgery.

Getting into Russia wasn't easy. There were problems with our visas and we ended up being delayed in Seattle, Washington. When we finally arrived in Russia, I was excited but also exhausted. It was on this trip that I spent my first night alone. The school was wonderful. Fred and I enjoyed teaching and I was quickly learning several Russian songs. However, our joy was short-lived. Early one morning, the students were startled by a surprise police visit. The police had come to the school the day before asking questions but we never expected that they would return at the crack of dawn. Our students, fearing for our safety told us to stay locked in our room, which we did. We heard all kinds of frightening noises, gunshots, and screams. Sitting quietly on the floor of our room we waited, not knowing what to do. The police tried multiple times to open and break down our door. After the fourth attempt, when they couldn't open it, they returned with a pry bar, determined to see what was behind the sealed door. One of our students distracted them and they left, arresting all of our students. Throughout this whole time, I had no fear. I had faced cancer and lived. I knew that God was with me and that He had a plan for my life. Surely everything would work out.

Eventually the pastor's wife came to rescue us. She drove us around, looking for a safe place for us to hide. The situation at the school looked bad and no one knew what the outcome would be. It was better for us to stay out of sight. Eventually, Fred and I realized that we would have to leave Russia. We stayed with some American friends until we could get a flight back to America. The conditions at the Bible School had been very bad. There had been no heat, no running water, no inside toilet. The food supply was minimal and it seemed like many of the students had bronchitis. Yet I was happy. I always wanted to be a missionary. I had fought a battle with cancer; I had given up everything to be a missionary in Russia; and now it was all over. Our hopes and dreams of becoming missionaries lasted for a mere two weeks. I was devastated.

The flight back to America was heartbreaking to say the least. I was holding back the tears when two men from California walked up to our seats and sat down next to us. They knew about our situation and had been praying for us. They began to tell us that we had not made a mistake by going to Russia, that God was pleased with our willingness to go, and that He had an even greater plan for our lives. The words were comforting, but it didn't change the fact that we had nothing to "go home to." Our new occupation was gone, we had resigned our church and that was gone, our house was gone and our son was gone. Everything was gone.

In less than one year's time, Fred and I had one stressful situation after another. We made four major mission trips. I survived cancer, surgery, and radiation. My great-aunt passed away. Our only son was in Bible School and we were struggling with the "empty nest". We changed occupations, sold our house, given away most of our possessions, moved to Russia, and lost our students to arrest. We had to hide in several places in Russia and eventually, even escape. Yes, it had been a hard year, but I wasn't about to give up. I cried my share of tears, gritted my teeth, put a smile on my face, and remembered the Apostle Paul who said, "Be watchful, stand firm in your faith, be courageous, be strong."[1]

We landed in Seattle, Washington and stayed there for a while just trying to recover from our ordeal in Russia. Then we flew back to New York and began traveling to family, friends, and a few churches, explaining the reality of "religious freedom" in the former Soviet Union. In the meantime, my dad was calling his good friend in Africa, Pastor Paul. He and Paul arranged for us to start a Bible school and live with him in Abidjan, Côte d'Ivoire, West Africa. Shortly after Christmas, we bought airplane tickets for Africa. On my first Sunday there, the pastor asked me to sing a special song for the church. I stood facing the congregation, a sea of unknown faces, and sang about the faithfulness of God. The date was February 3rd, exactly one year from my surgery.

The scenario may be different but the question that is demanded of you will remain the same. Will you give up? Will you go away? Will you leave? Those words asked in different ways, all mean the same thing. Will you break your covenant?

I couldn't give up. I could never leave God's house. The year had been hard but giving up and running away from home was not an option. I had entered into God's house by an eternal Covenant and I wasn't leaving. Some of my friends asked me how I could go on. Others wondered why I didn't quit. They would say things like, "How can you continue to serve God and pursue this mission dream, when everything seemingly keeps going wrong?" God had proven himself faithful to me. It was with confidence that I could stand and sing, on my first Sunday in Africa, the same song I had sung exactly one year earlier, "What A Faithful God Have I!"

We all have seasons when we would like to give up - maybe yours is a year, a day, a month, or even decades. The scenario may be different but the question that is demanded of you will remain the same. Will you give up? Will you go away? Will you leave? Those words asked in different ways, all mean the same thing. Will you break your covenant?

One day, my sister and I were lamenting about the discrepancies we saw in the body of Christ. Cheri, my sister, is the postmistress in a local post office. She has worked very hard to gain that position and has worked in many different locations. She is also the Administrative Pastor in a small church. She told me how shocked she was comparing what she saw happening at the post office and what happens in the church. She was surprised to see so many Christians leave and separate from their marriages, family relationships, and churches, whereas at the post office, people would stay year after year. She told me about people who hated their job at the post office. They hated the people with whom they worked and everything about the job, and yet day after day, year after year, they would come to work, never being late, even exchanging Christmas presents. They would give the job the best they could. Why? Because of their paycheck and retirement. These people were willing to ignore their offenses and disagreements for the almighty dollar.

Please don't misunderstand and think that I am saying that you can never escape difficult situations. I know that like

David and Saul, there are times when one has to leave a Covenant Relationship. However, you should think about the ramifications of leaving for a very long time before separating from your spouse, your friends, or church. Make sure that the reason you are leaving is because, like David, you have no other choice. Don't make leaving an easy solution. It should be the hardest decision of your life, one that you labor over with tears, fasting, and prayer. Know that even if you have no other choice, you and even your children will suffer the curse of the broken covenant.

A few years ago, a great men's movement was formed, called Promise Keepers. This group of men, from all walks of life, promised to remain faithful to their marriage. No matter what temptation came their way, they promised that they would not leave their wife. We need another movement like this for the entire body of Christ. The world needs people who will keep their promise and not leave families, friends, and churches. In every life, there are seasons when breaking Covenant seems like the only answer or the easy way out. The world needs people who, even in the most difficult times of their lives, will say, "I'm in this for the long haul. I shall not be moved. You can get me to leave my spouse, my friend, my church when, and only when, you pry my stone cold fingers off from them." If people will stay in a dead-end job for such temporal things as money or health insurance, or work with people they hate only to keep up with their neighbors, how much more should we, as the glorious body of Christ, remain in our Covenants. We have been promised eternal rewards for our faithfulness, not only for us, but for a thousand generations to follow.[2]

> **Deuteronomy 7:9** Know therefore that the LORD your God is God, the faithful God who keeps covenant and steadfast love with those who love him and keep his commandments, to a thousand generations, RSV

I have preached my Covenant messages in many churches, all over the world. Sometimes when I return to a church, I hear a sad and disturbing report. Sometimes, I find that the very people who listened and were so excited about Covenant, left their church, and caused a church split. Suffering the curse of broken Covenants, they now flounder in their marriage, family, and Christian walk. Don't let that person be you! The Bible says that we will *know* the truth and it will set us free. It's not enough to hear the truth. We have to *know* the truth. We need the truth to become a part of us, and get deep inside before it can change us. Freedom comes with a price, and that price is the living sacrifice that says, "I'm willing to be offended. I'm willing for my faith to be tried. I'm willing to pay any price that I might remain in my Covenant and stay in God's house. I *know* the truth and it has set me free."

The world needs people who, even in the most difficult times of their lives, will say, "I'm in this for the long haul. I shall not be moved.

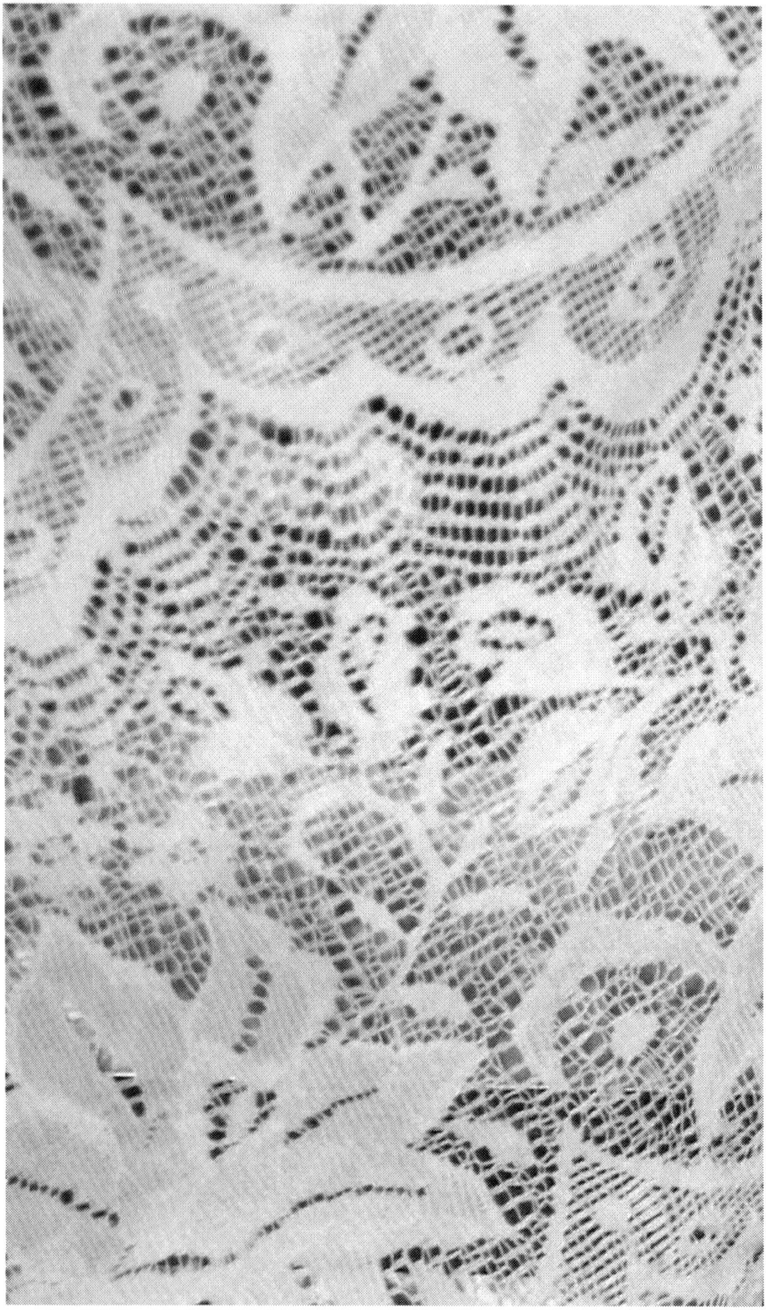

Chapter 16

The Bush Still Burns

Psalms 57:1-2 Be merciful to me, O God, be merciful to me! For my soul trusts in You; And in the shadow of Your wings I will make my refuge… I will cry out to God Most High, To God who performs all things for me. NKJV

"What a beautiful day it was," Moses thought. He had been taking care of his father-in-law's sheep for so long, that the days seemed to blur into one another. But today, well, the sunbeams seemed to come straight from heaven. Why, even the bushes looked like they were glowing with a heavenly fire. Fire? Moses turned and gave it a closer inspection. At that very moment God began to speak to him.

"Moses!"

"Is someone speaking to me?" Moses asked as he peered deeper into the burning bush. Who was that speaking? "God? Is that you?"

Imagine the thoughts that must have run through Moses' mind. God was speaking to him. Yes, he was once a great prince in Egypt, but now he was a lowly shepherd. He had spoken to Pharaoh and the greatest leaders of his day. But it had been years since anyone of importance had noticed him. Why would the great God of the universe speak to him? This is much like the question David asked years later, "God, is this the way you deal with man? Why have you chosen me?"[1]

When we came to Almighty God and made an everlasting Covenant with Him, we made our home in His house. Through the wonder of Covenant, God then made His home in us.

Isaiah 55:3 Incline your ear, and come to Me. Hear, and your soul shall live; And I will make an everlasting covenant with you—The sure mercies of David. NKJV

God has chosen to make a Covenant with both you and I. **Isaiah 55:3** says that God will make an everlasting Covenant with us. What a wonderful thought. God Almighty in an everlasting Covenant with us. He not only makes the Covenant; He wants it, and He wills it. Jesus even said in **Luke 12:15** that He eagerly desired the Covenant. What was this wonderful thing that Jesus desired? He desired a Covenant not of works but a Covenant of grace, which is an everlasting Covenant. Jesus is our Covenant Redeemer and He makes us partakers of His grace. We have all the blessings and benefits of this Covenant.

The bush burned to facilitate the voice of God. There was a fire in that bush that compelled Moses to look and hear, and yet the bush was not consumed. Shadrach, Meshach, and Abednego were thrown into a fiery furnace, yet they were not consumed. Not only that, but the presence of God was with them, walking, talking, and changing their lives. The Gibeonites were instructed, according to their Covenant, to keep the tabernacle fire going. They tended the fire, being changed in its presence, and were not consumed. Like these great men, we also have the privilege of being in the presence of the fire of God. Instead of being consumed by the fire, it changes us forever.

When we came to Almighty God and made an everlasting Covenant with Him, we made our home in His house. Through the wonder of Covenant, God then made His home in us. We are the temple of the Living God and His fire now burns in us.[2] Like the Gibeonites we now have the awesome responsibility to keep the blaze burning. Moses didn't have to make God work in his life; Moses' purpose was fulfilled as he obeyed God. David didn't have to make God crown him as the king of Israel; David's purpose was fulfilled as he worshiped God. Honoring their Covenant with God these great men kept the fire burning. You and I don't have to make things happen in our lives, we just have to keep the fire of God burning by loving, trusting, honoring, and obeying the Lord God, our Covenant Redeemer. As the fire burns, God speaks and works His purposes in us.

As he approached Goliath, David said, "I am going to kill you today. Then all of the world will know that there is a God who lives in Israel." God desires to do great things in our lives so all the world will know that He lives in us. God wants to adopt us into His family, not only for the world to see Him living in us, but that we also have our home in Him. He desires us not to be hopeless slaves, but lovers of Covenant, so that all of the world would know that He lives in us. God chooses to be our Covenant Redeemer so that all of the world would see, and know who He is, by looking at our lives. He looks for us; He cares about the smallest details; He chooses to be in an everlasting Covenant that forgives us and welcomes us into His home.

None of us should look back at past mistakes, hurts, or disappointments. We need to look forward to what God has promised through His Covenant. The Covenant tells us that the past is forgiven and forgotten. We cannot look back. It destroys our purpose. All that is required of us is to remain in the house, and to look forward to God.

Once, during my senior year in high school, while riding the school bus, I saw a younger girl who was crying. I didn't know the girl very well but I wondered what was wrong, so I sat down next to her. I asked her why she was crying and she told me that she thought she was pregnant. She was afraid of being a single mother but more than that, she felt very alone. That morning, she had told her father about her pregnancy. He cursed as he told her that she was "good for nothing" and then informed her that she shouldn't bother coming home after school. She finished her sad tale by saying, "I don't know what to do. I have no place to go."

I responded immediately, "After school today, you'll come home with me."

It never occurred to me that I should first ask my mom and dad before inviting someone home with me. Of course, if someone were in trouble, my mom and dad would help them. So, as soon as school was over, my new friend and I rode the school bus to my house. After we arrived, I told my parents about my friend's problems and they talked with her for quite a while. Soon she was tucked into bed sleeping the sleep of one who had just given her troubles to someone older and wiser.

Later that night after everyone else had gone to bed, my father called me aside. I wondered if I were in trouble for inviting someone home without permission. However, as soon as my dad began speaking, I realized that I could not have been more wrong. With great love in his eyes he said, "Debby, I want you to always remember what I am about to tell you. Your mom and I love you very much and no matter what you may do, no matter how many mistakes you have made, you can always come home." These same words resound from our loving Heavenly Father. Open your heart and listen to Him as He says, "Child, I love you. No matter what you may do, no matter how many mistakes you have made, you can always come home. You can ALWAYS come home."

The Only Way Out Is In.

"Child, I love you. No matter what you may do, no matter how many mistakes you have made you can always come home. You can ALWAYS come home."

Resources

1. H Clay Trumbull
   Salt Covenant
   Blood Covenant
   Threshold Covenant

2. Matthew Pools Commentary
3. Microsoft® Encarta® Reference Library 2002. © 1993-2001 Microsoft Corporation. All rights reserved.

4. John Gills Works:
   An Exposition of the Old and NEW TESTAMENT, THE WHOLE ILLUSTRATED WITH NOTES, TAKEN FROM THE MOST ANCIENT JEWISH WRITINGS.
   BY JOHN GILL, D.D.
   LONDON:
   PRINTED FOR MATHEWS AND LEIGH, 18 STRAND,
   by W. Clowes, Northumberland-Court
   1809

   Edited and revised and updated
   by Larry Pierce, 1994-1995.

   Assisted by Tom Cox, Earnie Stefanik, Paul Houghton,
   and Peter Robinson, and Jay Sklar,
   and Damaris Martin, Kerri Playford and Lori Hoffman,
   and others.

Foot Notes

Preface

1. Hebrews 7:18; 8:6-13

Chapter 1

1. Adapted from story in **Make a note of who the author is and some more information in appendage**. .*Threshold Covenant* page 4
2. *Threshold Covenant* pg 5
3. *Threshold Covenant pg 94*
4. Threshold Covenant page 139-147

Chapter 2

1. 1 Samuel 17:32.GILLS: Josephus says… and the wounded of the Philistines fell…thirty thousand, and twice as many wounded
2. Deuteronomy 30:12-16
3. Deuteronomy 28:7; 30:7
4. Joshua 5
5. Acts 13:22
6. I Samuel 17:45-46
7. Matthew 22:36
8. Strongs 1451

Chapter 3

1. Threshold Covenant page 59, Exodus 21:5, 6
2. Deuteronomy 30:6; Colossians 2:11-14
3. Romans 5:5; (Lord's Work Trust, Deuteronomy 1; Online Bible, CH McIntosh) Romans 5:5
4. Gills Psalms 34:18
5. Revelation 3:20
6. Romans 1:1; Ephesians 3:1; 4:1; 2 Timothy 1:8; Philemon 1:1,9

Chapter 4

1. Threshold Covenant pg 19-20
2. Ezekiel 47:1
3. Luke 15:11
4. Leviticus 7:21
5. Luke 15:22 Gills Notes

6. Luke 15:23 Adam Clarks Commentary

Chapter 5

1. Exodus 12:7
2. Deut 29:5
3. Threshold Covenant page 188 Trumbull
4. Trumbull…page 67-85 Threshold Covenant
5. See Trumbull page 68
6. Trumbull page 75
7. Threshold Covenant Page 9
8. H.C. Trumbull Threshold Covenant Page 199
9. Romans 7:15

Chapter 6

1. Gills notes on Gilgal
2. Joshua 21:17, 28; Joshua 21:13-19; 1 Chronicles 8:29-33; 1 Chronicles 9:35; 1 Kings 3:4-5; Jeremiah 28:1
3. Matthew Pools Commentary Matthew 5:14
4. John Winthrop….Microsoft® Encarta® Reference Library 2002. © 1993-2001 Microsoft Corporation. All rights reserved.
5. Deuteronomy 4:20; 9:26,29

Chapter 7

1. Gills Notes Joshua 10

Chapter 8

1. Name has been changed
2. Gills John 10:1
3. Threshold Covenant Trumble page 231-233
4. Galatians 3:1
5. Romans 4:16; 5:15; 11:6; 8:1-15; Ephesians 2:8
6. Hebrews 11:1
7. *HarrowSchool, 29 October 1941*

Chapter 9

1. The Land Registration Act 2002
2. James 4:7
3. Matthew 14:43-45
4. Matthew 21:12; Mark 11:15
5. Gills notes Mark 11:15
6. Ephesians 4:26
7. NIV Study Bible footnote Genesis 1:5

8. Matthew 17:21; Mark 9:29

Chapter 10

1. Gills notes on Ruth 1:4
2. Ruth 4:18-22
3. Matthew 12:34
4. Deuteronomy 28:13
5. Phil 3:14
6. 1 Corinthians 15:19

Chapter 11

1. 1 Samuel 15:22
2. 1 Samuel 28:16
3. Psalms 139:7

Chapter 12

1. Galatians 4
2. 1 Samuel 20:32
3. 2 Samuel 11
4. 2 Chronicles 13:5
5. Daniel 3
6. Hebrews 13:5
7. Matthew 1:6

Chapter 13

1. Romans 8:28
2. Deuteronomy 11:26-28

Chapter 14

1. Acts 16

Chapter 15

1. 1 Corinthians 16:13
2. Deuteronomy 7:9; Psalms 105:8

Chapter 16

1. 1 Chronicles 17:16
2. 2 Corinthians 6:16